D1715119

Revealed in the birth moment of the horoscope is the "expanded present" of an individual's whole future. With this volume begins Noel Tyl's examination of the horoscope extended in time—an examination aimed ultimately at aiding the individual in finding his place in the "inexorable flow of time."

The author clarifies the main techniques of prediction: radix methods, rapport measurements, Secondary Progressions, and his own discovery, factor-7 time-scan. He lays out useful procedures for quickly estimating and corroborating important developments in the horoscope, so that they can be checked by more precise measurements. His approach strengthens the deductive reasoning capacities of every astrologer.

The author shows that the various systems of prediction, though each alone is partial in its approach to measuring future potential, can in concert suggest it—much as the number of tangents on the cover of this book can begin to hint at the perfection of the circle.

The Expanded Present

Volume VI

The Principles and Practice
of Astrology

The Llewellyn Syllabus
for home study and college curriculum

The Principles and Practice
of Astrology

Noel Tyl

A complete text for instruction and reference in the practice of
standard astrological methods and the psychological and
philosophical principles for analysis and application. In 12 volumes.

The Expanded Present
Radix Methods and Secondary Progressions

1974
Llewellyn Publications
Saint Paul, Minnesota, 55165, U.S.A.

First Edition 1974

Llewellyn Publications
Post Office Box 3383
Saint Paul, Minnesota 55165

International Standard Book Number: 0-87542-805-3
Library of Congress Catalog Card Number: 73-19923

Printed in the United States of America

This certainly seems to be
in the nature of a miracle,
the mode of which
surpasses the human understanding,
although no one who is not ignorant of astrology
may doubt its truth.

Jean Baptiste Morin
(1583-1656)
Astrologia Gallica

Contents

1

The Dilemma

Prediction represents only the apex of a massive pyramid of astrological knowledge. Prediction is grounded upon the analytical synthesis of horoscope potentials: the Sun-Sign; the needs that guide personality formation, represented by the Moon; the Ascendant's representation of Self to others; the mental processes, the sociability and emotions, the application of energy, the enthusiasms and opportunities, the ambition, the workings of the inner Self: the unconscious, suggesting individuality, vision, and a perspective within the world. A system emerges, a composition, that indicates potential. The parts organize themselves within a law of naturalness, grounded upon family environment, opportunities for education and experience, the expansion of personal horizon into professional focus within society, the fulfillment of dreams, a recognition of destiny. Patterns of need and response are created. —Only when this grand base is understood, can a projection into the future be made, a prediction supported by the base of rich understanding.

Throughout his history, man has had a fascination

with the nature of prediction. All students and professional astrologers alike dream of penetrating the mysteries, of finding the way and the courage to project Astrology into the future and help man toward maximum fulfillment. The building of the base leads to the apex—and to a dilemma: the relative ease with which we can analyze the past and discuss inherent potentials, only to collide with a wall of inhibition and insecurity when it comes to expanding our analyses to include future time. We wonder how far we can go, how far we should go; when we analyze a horoscope, we wonder when does the future begin, when does the apex begin to form itself. —The dilemma really stems from two concerns: the concept of man's natural integrity and the concept of time.

Man's integrity. The word *integrity* has two meanings. The first is wholeness, completeness, implying a definite self-sufficiency; the second is honesty, purity. Together, the meanings fuse to represent man's natural wholeness, his endowment through creation. For Christianity, man is whole and complete, created in the image and likeness of God. For all religions, man lives to develop himself to a higher station defined by a god-theory. Psychologically, man works to self-completion through fulfillment of potentials. —When man inspects his life, he can analyze mistakes made along the way to development in the past. His present is the bridge to fresh opportunities in the future. Dare anyone . . . another mortal involved in the same life-endeavor. . .intrude upon man's right to grow at a rate and in a direction he discovers for himself?

In the reality of creation, man gains autonomous importance. Man has always presumed this integrity and self-importance: he has erect posture; he can make things; he can think to outwit other creatures; he can interpret nature; the gods walk with him. Religions say that, in the beginning, perhaps in the Age of *Leo*-Aquarius, the gods, the god-will became men. In the *Antigone,* Sophocles wrote the ringing chorus: "many a creature lives, but none mightier than man." —At the dawn of the Age of Aquarius, man expresses the precessed polarity of *Aquarius*-Leo by finding the God *within himself.* Man's science details man's environment, reveals the whole of which he is part. Knowledge expands his integral completeness. Social structures protect the individual's rights. Individual freedoms are stressed continuously. The integral ego is king.

There are strong kings and weak kings. The strong ones may embrace any help they can get to improve their position, embellishing their completeness. Or they may reject any help at all—"to be surprised by the future"—in order to show their strength in meeting new challenges. The weak ones may reject help in fear that weaknesses may be discovered. "Kings" of different Sun-Signs express their integrity, weakly or strongly, in different modes: the Cardinal Signs are prepared to take charge of new development; the Fixed Signs are prepared to meet development head-on, to take it as it comes; the Mutable Signs are ever ready to cooperate with development and assimilate it through reaction.

Prediction is an invasion of the ego's privacy, the

king's integral domain. So is analysis of his past; the latter is more tolerable because the past is a matter of record. But, in terms of integrity, should one man allow another to intrude; should an astrologer presume that he can? The problem is intensified by the fact that man and astrologer are the same; they are men in life together. In ancient times, prophets, seers, oracles, soothsayers were given special social positions. They seemed to have a special talent and were assimilated into society and put to work by the kings of the day. The planet-gods were beside man on the battlefields and in the market place. It was man's respectable privilege to communicate with the god-personages through individuals who had an inside track.

In modern times, every man is a king unto himself. The planet-gods and their activity have become esoteric formulae, removed by science from everyday life. The prophet, the inside track, has been supplanted by scientific reason: man's science harnesses nature for man's use. Education increases extravagantly every man's potentials. Modern man is very, very proud indeed.

With refined skills (his own scientific reason), seasoned courage (his own cultivated experience), and sensitivity (his awareness of the dilemma), the astrologer *does* presume to predict. His ethic must be to build an informative relationship between himself and other men. Together, *integrity is further defined:* man's completeness is given dynamic time perspective.

Time. Is time absolute? —Before Einstein, science

claimed that indeed it was, and anyone who worked with the future violated a natural, "scientific" barrier. But the theory of relativity reversed this thesis, stating that time and space are different aspects of the same reality, that time is *a property of the "world" in which it is measured. Each individual has his own time awareness, his own development "space."* In modern thought, what *is* absolute about time is its *flow,* its continuance. Man's sensibilities consume the present. Presents become pasts and renew themselves within a future.

Man's problem with time is a problem of his consciousness, his activity within life space, within the flow of duration. Man's unconscious is not aware of time barriers: he dreams easily of the past, the future, and other "worlds."

Theories have been presented that there is no separation between past and future, that all-time exists, and that man's concept of duration is only a clarification of focus, gradated progressively away from the most clear central point called the present. Mind-twisting hypotheses using the theory of relativity can logically prove a changing of subjective time sense when man is taken out of his normal objective world. Precognition in dreams constantly defies a time barrier and assimilates a future condition.

Scientific integrity requires the dimension of *reliability,* predictability: something will behave in a certain way under certain conditions every time these conditions occur. Science cites research in the past to justify a projection into the inevitable future. *To project* is to ride with the inexorable flow, out of the past portion of time into the future portion; but *to predict* is to spring from one moment in the flow to another yet to come. The arched spring is thought to ignore the intermediate flow and seems to introduce potential error by bridging the causal relationships yet to be accumulated.

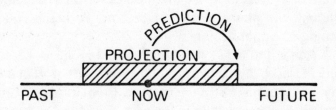

For example: a businessman can project his rise in his company during the next two years. He projects his past performance into the future; he rides his time flow within his development space. His projection carries with it an expectation of performance that has already been established in the past. The projection would be "If I keep going at this rate, I should be regional manager in two years."

Now, a prediction could be made through Astrology that he will not be with the company in two years, that he will not last! For reasons shown in the horoscope, his time with the company would come to a halt. A new time-construct would begin with another company. The prediction, defying the projection, would consequently appear improbable, even absurd.

If the prediction were made that this businessman would indeed become regional manager in two years, the prediction, corresponding to his own projection, would not seem very dramatic. —So often, it seems that prediction is expected to include dramatic change somehow; but a projection acknowledges natural evolvement.

If it were uncovered that the executive had a past history of frequent job changes, the prediction would become more tenable, *appear more like a projection because the past had proved the possibility.*

This distinction between projection and prediction is very subtle. A wall is erected against the unexpected, the occurrence not obviously programmed into the integral order of the past. —Yet, to the astrologer, *prediction and projection are really almost always the same.* Rarely can an astrologer make a reliable prediction without seeing it as a projection of native potentials and the horoscopic past. He works with and from the beginning of time, the birth moment. The flow of time for the astrologer neither stops nor begins with the present. For the astrologer, the diagram on page 6 is different:

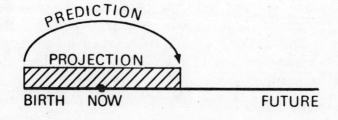

One should never forget that the concept of prophecy includes *interpretation* as well as prediction. The prophets of the Bible interpreted the "signs" from God. Astrologers interpret signs not dissimilar. The meaning of life in time is to develop, to improve our gift of creation. The moment of birth records every heavenly dimension, every "sign" of our endowment.

Being human, we are inhibited as astrologers. Who are we to have an inside track? Do we commit hubris by presuming a nearness to the timing of creation's unfolding, by "playing god"? Our sobriety must be maintained by refining our skills, seasoning our courage with experience, and sensitizing our communication with other men living within the same mystery. The future is our challenge. Yet, the future is our fear because it contains an existential end. Prophecy is our interpretation of the past and our projection into the fullness of time.

Who predicts, and how? Everyone predicts. Predictions in the present *seem to help time advance*. The man who can see no future for himself begins to die. The man who can see where he is going has everything to live for. —What is the "power of positive thinking"?

Stock brokers predict continuously for their clients, doctors for their patients, politicians and political observers for their nations. Almost invariably, the predictions of these specialists are based upon analyses of past trends and reactions projected forward into the inevitable future, upon the time-flow. Should they just spring ahead into the future with a prediction, the prediction is called a "hunch" and is socially acceptable because it admits possible error. If the hunch pays off, the person becomes a genius speculator, a prophet!

Just as brokers, doctors, and politicians are specialists, applying measurements that relate to special departments in life, so is the astrologer a specialist. But the astrologer works with measurements and "symptoms" that go through *all* departments of life to develop an overall pattern. Financial, medical, or political astrologers specialize in certain areas of the pattern.

So, another part of the prediction dilemma comes from this area of specialization: the doctor can advise the broker about his *health;* the broker can advise the doctor about his *finances.* But the broker would not tell the doctor anything about medicine, and rarely can a doctor be as eminently credible about stocks as the broker is. —Yet, the astrologer presumes to advise all, broker, doctor, and Indian chief about their life patterns. The astrologer is often thought to invade their completeness when *he is only defining it further within time.* He has all the facts too, but his "facts," his techniques are often not widely known or appreciated; they often collide with scientific concepts and human integrity—in the opinion of those who know nothing of Astrology.

Astrologers predict with esoteric techniques, techniques not known by or easily shared with many people. Astrology is a scientific art form linked with the intangible considerations of existence. To safeguard and improve the stature of Astrology, we must be extremely careful with prediction. There is an enormous tendency to overdo Astrology, to show off, to find a place in the Sun through dramatic prophecy. How many times has the end of the world been predicted? —and by reputable astrologers too! How often do publicized predictions seem to fail? —What we say and how we say it is Astrology's stock report, its bill of health.

The major security for an astrologer's prediction is found in his full understanding of his client's potentials, shown in the birth horoscope, and in his full inspection of his client's reactions in the past. Potentials and reactions form the base of the pyramid. Many predictions that fail suggest a neglect of this base. With transits and the progressed Moon particularly (page 75), inaccurate predictions can be avoided by seeking out the same or similar planetary configuration in the past and learning the client's reaction then to guide interpretation of reaction in the future. Note that advisors to world statesmen today are most often *historians,* seeking to understand government and life in the past to project deduced development and cycles into the future.

Free will and fate. From the twin stem of the prediction dilemma, integrity and time, grows the grand consideration of free will and fate. The view of human integrity embodies the essence of free will, the dimensions of self-initiation. The view of time contains considerations of fate, the dimension of preordained potentials and circumstances. Integral man vacillates between I-create-my-future-myself and my-future-is-created-for-me. Man uses one concept or the other *to suit his momentary condition.* One concept or the other can encourage or explain a given moment. Free will is used to explain success; fate, to explain difficulty.

Man often neglects the vital third cooperating concept: *the concept of level,* the dimension of quality. Man brings his free will forward in time with each new moment of life. He consumes the future and the experiences that may be mysteriously set beforehand. He can use his will within fate to adjust his *level of acceptance* of the future.

In many senses, man is a magnet. He attracts time and experience, opportunities for self-fulfillment. He can be a strong magnet or a weak one... admired, valued, outdated, discarded, used-up, etc. The same mysterious rapport among the planets includes the Earth and life upon it. Man's degree of magnetism (as a focal point of time and space experiences) varies during his life, naturally and through applied knowledge, to the degree that he *can* often seem *to make things happen!*—to attract opportunity or to repel it. He makes things happen as observably and inscrutably as *planets* make things happen!

The discussion of fate and free will is endless. It spreads easily to include psychological nuance and philosophical argument. It varies with every individual, and, indeed, the management of free will, fate, and level *is* individuality. *—For astrologers, sympathy with the dilemma brings respectability to inquiry, caution to deduction, and poise to presentation.*

The Expanded Present. The present itself has no

duration, no measureable existence. It is difficult to postulate a separate division between future and present, between apex and pyramid. The past is sure; it defines flow and promises a future. To stabilize himself existentially, man *constructs* a present. The present becomes now, today, yesterday and today, last week and this week, last year and this year, etc. The construction of the present expands; it includes a portion of the past *and* a portion of the future. *The more secure man is, the broader his construction of the present:* his will in present application gains more control over fate in expanded time.

An example: when a student studies for an examination, his present is intensified. Time seems to take on different dimensions: there might not be enough time; time might seem to flow too quickly or slow down enormously. The present involved with studying is expanded to include the examination due in the future, the next day, the next week, the next month. The ground he must cover in his study—review of past studies—and the time set for the examination determine the breadth of the study-present. That present expands to cover a portion of the past and a portion of the future. The student projects from along this line and within this frame of the expanded present. He uses his will to prepare for his fate. He uses his time efficiently if he prepares to meet his future at a level as high as his inherent potentials will allow. —The concept of fate says only that he *will have the examination.* Free will and native potentials determine the level of his performance.

Man expands the present to give meaning to

endeavor. The housewife justifies her cooking early in the morning for a party that night. For her, the party later begins with the preparations now. A businessman can justify his work by his plans for retirement security. For him, the accumulated benefits later begin with the preparations now. Religions give meaning to life as a preparation for a Second Coming or rebirth. The construction of this philosophical present even transcends interruptions by death.

Astrologers expand the present. We go back as far as possible: to the moment of birth. We work with the client's own expanded present: his hopes, self-justifications, projections. We gather information for our study of life development. We measure capabilities and effectiveness of will. We assimilate the dimensions of the dilemma. We participate in time and give meaning to a strategically expanded present.

Causality. Since time immemorable, man has felt that he is the subject most worthy of his own study: to defend himself against other creatures, to exploit nature, to live more comfortably with other men, and—most important—to reason somehow the why and how of existence. All around him, man sees cause and effect. Philosophically, this is dependence and contingency. Things "must be" linked together. Only skepticism denies all links. Theologically, man wrestles with thought and theory to prove that he is necessary, that he is an effect of some cause. Proving this would remove his anxiety, his fear of not-being. He seeks to delineate his function in objective terms of cause and effect, motive and manifestation, within the flow of time.

Rationalists have held that the link between cause and effect is some intrinsic feature in the nature of things. Again, there is the notion of necessity linking things in certain ways, man included. Every philosopher has attacked the problem. Aristotle suggested several conditions within causality: matter, form, efficiency, and finality; i.e., the substance of the thing, its condition in time and space, the trigger-focus working upon it, and the motive-goal of the response. Locke and Hume studied considerations of *resemblance* in causality: contiguous occurrence in space and time, association from habit, and adjustment of effects. Kierkegaard's existentialism (in response to Hegel's objective idealism) emphasized the need for man to act and choose from a spontaneous function of the will, answerable only to God—this was the divine cause within the soul.

In man's earliest days, his awe of the heavens was translated into causal theory: man was the substance in human condition; the environment worked upon him; motive-goals struggled for fulfillment. In later times, with the gods removed from the immediate environment, spiritual causality was ignored *or* emphasized, causes were fortuitous and habitual or incarnated and inspired. —Throughout all these times, the astrologers among men observed a cooperation between man on Earth and the planets in the heavens. The planets were in motion within time. The parallel between these motions and man's development within the same time became cause and effect . . . condition, trigger, motive.

Causation created tension within man's sense of his own will as he grew in sophistication and accumulated knowledge. If he couldn't do anything about his life, the integrity of his will was threatened, he was impotent, less individual. Yet doing "something" introduced the possibility of doing the wrong thing, the thing that altered the cause somehow to bring a negative effect. The concept of sin or wrong-doing was introduced, held by Augustine not as a material principle in nature but as the outcome of a bad will. Guilt was born and complicated further our responsibility within the great cause-and-effect mystery.

The psychologist-philosopher, Carl Gustav Jung suggested a concept of *synchronicity* to help explain causality. Astrologers have adopted this explanation to achieve a practical peace: there is no causal relationship between the heavens and Earth. Rather, there is a parallel in time, *a correspondence of development.* As above, so below. Developments occur within man on Earth as corresponding developments occur among the planets in heaven.

We know that the Moon is linked with the tides on Earth. There is a definite correspondence. Yet, we do not know the nature of the correspondence, the force. Gravity cannot be explained as yet. —Causal concepts are argued to find an answer to make man more comfortable existentially. Man thinks, therefore he exists. He can doubt everything except that he *does* think. Why he thinks is unanswerable. What he thinks is demonstrable through the effects his thoughts cause, the experiences he "attracts."

To improve our comfort within the dilemma of causation, we can seek only to adjust effect by preparing our will, to anticipate effect by rearranging conditions within our necessary time. This is the work of Astrology.

Astrologers map the moment of birth. It is an imprint of the moment that has eternal validity. That moment includes past inheritance and future potential. The unfolding of the potentials symbolized in the horoscope creates an architecture of life, a pyramid of being. As the construction grows, we can inspect its progress. In time, we can bring discipline to the construction, manipulating variables to achieve the highest level of development. Our disciplines become systems, ever attempting to give form and predictability to mystery, to provide man with his due glory in fulfillment at his apex.

2

Formulating Prediction Systems
—Not a Simple Matter!

The birth horoscope is man's first moment of time within his world, his development space. This time is within other times; this place is within other places. There is a relativity factor among the times, among the places. There is a relativity factor between man and the cosmos. As we have seen, the symbol of the Sun states this relativity: the circle of the solar system with man at its center. In Astrology, we work with an Earth-center, a human center, and we view the solar system revolving around this center. Man's position in space and time is not only *contained* within the positioning of the entire system, it is emphasized at its center.

The study of Astrology is dedicated to understanding this relativity between heaven and man (Earth), between the macrocosm and the microcosm. Man uses his systems of logic and numbers to capture the order, to understand *his* time within *other* times, *his* place within *other* places. Mathematics provides a functional description; philosophy attempts a reasonable comprehension. *—But neither the mathematics nor the philosophy is perfect, has the key, is*

17

fulfilled in knowledge of the whole. There is a factor of indeterminateness that pervades nature, that indeed keeps man in his place. Man cannot find the beginning of the circle, nor the process of its curve. He knows only his center and relationship to the space around him.

Movement as symbol of development. Movement is a function of time and space. In time, a seed unfolds, grows upward in space to reach the Sun, develops in individual color, shape, and function.

The birth horoscope describes the seed. It records the first moment, the imprint of potential, the placement in time and space of the "I." The planetary symbols of this imprint begin to unfold, to move in space and time. "I am" occurs—the process of becoming. Growth takes place to fulfill the individual Sun.

The symbolic meanings of the planets were established to a great extent by their speeds and distances from the Sun. These symbolic meanings in the birth chart establish the life-potentials developed in astrological synthesis. The miracle of birth and the investiture with potentials carry with them the need to grow and the responsibility to fulfill. The new-born moves into life-awareness. Development in life begins immediately. The symbols of the identity move in time and space; the dimensions of the personality develop in parallel.

Astrological theorists have long sought a key relativity factor within the dimensions of celestial movement to define the dimensions of human development. —The parallels abounded: there are 360 degrees in the circle, 365 days in the solar year; there are four seasons (the horoscope Angles) and a new degree of the Zodiac rising over the horizon every four minutes, one whole cycle of the Zodiac completed in one day by the axial rotation of the Earth; the Moon's orbit around the Earth is completed in almost one month. The relativity factors are *almost* exact: close enough to motivate study; disparate enough to baffle inquiry.

Investigation pursued the relationship between time-space wholes, the integral parts within the grand whole of cosmic harmony. The Earth's orbit around the Sun gave the Sun an apparent motion that completed *exposure* to the whole vault of the heavens, the Zodiac, *in one year*. The Earth's rotation upon its own axis once in each day gave complete *exposure* to the whole *in one day*. The macrocosm-microcosm thesis urged equation of these two motions which are used to construct the horoscope: intriguingly valid appeared the equations of *one year equals one degree; one year equals one day*.

The ancients had relied upon observable conjunctions between planets, eclipses, comets, and a legacy of augury to make predictions. In the middle ages, extensive tables of motion were created to aid in predicting these important conjunctions and celestial phenomena ahead of time. However, the tables of motion were still unreliable. Predictions failed. Debates among the learned abounded. Attention was refocused upon the birth horoscope as singularly valid for character delineation—and prediction. The equation one year = one degree gained prominence. Astrologers would take the Sun, Moon, Ascendant, or

Midheaven (and often the Part of Fortune) as *significator* and measure the degree-distance to another important planet in the birth horoscope, called the *promissor*. If the distance between the significator Sun and promissor Saturn were twenty-eight degrees, a certain promised effect would be achieved by the conjunction within the life-experience of the twenty-eighth year.

This system was close but not exact: the 360-degree circle does not exactly fit the 365-day year; the latitudes and declinations of the planets had not been observed. The so-called *arc of direction* was in one plane, while the path of the significator or the position of the promissor could be in quite another plane. Adjustments were made, equating one year with fifty-nine degrees and eight seconds, the average daily motion of the Sun; spherical trigonometry assimilated the variables of latitude and declination. —These systems are called the *radix system* and *primary directions*. Both have been further refined and changed, but still demand further study and observation.[1]

Around 1700, a method equating one year of life to *one day after birth* gained prominence. With the Keplerian Tables of motion, *actual* planetary positions *after* birth were used to calculate man's development of potentials within time. Using one day after birth for one year was called *Secondary Progressions*. Using actual planetary postions in future time was called *transits*.

Still—with many refinements and intersystem

1. The spherical trigonometric primary directions are not popular in modern astrological practice because of their cumbersome calculation. An authoritative text is recommended in the Appendix for the student's exploration.

cooperation—the relativity factor between heavenly movement and human development is elusive. Man's number system and philosophical reasoning cannot grasp the order of nature precisely. In a circle, the ratio of circumference to diameter is a constant, value pi, but man in his need to translate this relationship into an exact numerical equivalent is unable to do so. Even to the 100,000 decimal places compiled by modern computer systems, 3.14159—, there seems to be no pattern to the digits and no end. The symbolic perfection of pi can be *grasped* but not *equated* to man's number system. *But exercise of the system as far as it goes gives an order to our use of a symbolic relationship.* —The ever-recurring margin of difference in the study of natural order underlines the mystery of life and the margin of error as man attempts to lift the veil.

Through such systems, Astrology tries to define the process of life shown in the circle of the horoscope; the straight lines of Astrology's deductive reasoning make multiple tangents to the circle; in their multiple approaches, they *suggest* the whole.

Transcending indeterminateness. With enough straight lines, the circle appears. The greater the number of lines, the more clearly is the circle defined. Astrologers bring as many lines of study, analysis, and deduction as possible to the horoscope to define more clearly its wholeness of existence and development. Lines come not only from formal Astrological knowledge but, as well, from psychology, religion, sociology, medicine, economics, history, the occult, and other areas. Yet, no system can displace approximation with certitude. Comprehension is always a matter of degree.

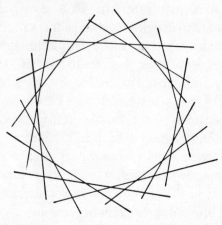

We can apply the macrocosm-microcosm thesis further to say that the indeterminateness of the natural order applies to the order in man as well: just as we cannot totally capture the exact significance of the natural order, we cannot totally capture the exact significance of man in his individual development. This is a return to the integrity dilemma, and it is the core of all criticism of Astrology throughout history: since no system is demonstratively perfect all the time, the astrologer must incorporate an element of himself, a fallible human dimension, to transcend indeterminateness in analysis. —It seems that the indeterminateness of the natural order is compounded by the indeterminateness of the human psyche.

Indeterminate man works with his own systems to grasp indeterminate nature. The integrity of Astrology is based upon each individual's degree of refinement within these systems and processes of deduction. This refinement is achieved through the function of awareness.

A mother, separated from her son geographically, without any actual knowledge of her son's condition, may suddenly *know* that he is ill or in danger. This is not intuition; it is a keen awareness—not a hunch, but a viscerally known phenomenon ... a knowing... inexplicable, indeterminate, but, somehow, organically valid. The mother's awareness is a phenomenon similar to the astrologer's awareness when he studies a horoscope: the son is a time and space continuum that emerged out of the mother, that exists as part of her, yet separately; the horoscope is a time and space continuum within the astrologer's awareness of the whole.

Awareness elevates; a lookout high on the mast of a ship is able to see around the bend of the river. Elevated awareness is a change in time and space positions. Awareness is a refinement of logic and systematic approximation. Awareness lifts systems to a higher level of application and comprehension.

Long study of Astrology—of the indeterminate—accustoms astrologers to the mystery. Long observation of the human-celestial experience refines interpretation and prediction potential. In our studies now, we will begin to cultivate awareness within development time and space. Each student will find his way, will identify personally with the systems. Each student will find his position to look ahead upon the mast. One will feel his awareness heightened by Secondary

Progressions; another, by Transits; another, by a combination of the two. A personal style will emerge, and the art of Astrology will be revealed.

The major systems introduced in this volume all seek to measure an expanded present from the birth moment to the present and beyond. Through these systems, the arc of the expanded present enables the astrologer, grounded upon the relationship between time and past experience as represented in the birth moment, to project into time.

The birth horoscope, as the seed plan of potentials, is entirely subjective in reference until time and space afford duration and development. As we move by means of analytical systems away from the birth moment, from radix methods through progressions to transits, subjective potentials are brought to objective challenge. The arc of the ever-expanding present carries with it microcosmic inclinations to be fulfilled in macrocosmic perspective. The arc is measured by the astrologer in several different ways to define its curve and to fill its vault with meaning. Systems and awareness work together to illuminate the natural relativity. The arc defines the process of becoming, of relationship, of meeting the world in the emergence of Self.

3

Awareness of Potential

Radix Methods

In our studies so far, the birth horoscope, called the *radix* (adjective: "radical"), has been viewed as static. No mention has been made of planetary movement or personality development. Since life is a fulfillment of the time and space imprint described by the radix, we gain a higher awareness of potential by inspecting the radix more carefully for the changes that we know will come after birth.

The planets move at different speeds. Some are in retrograde motion, appearing to move backwards. When two planets are in aspect together, one will be moving faster than the other, the aspect relationship between them will be increasing (*applying*) or diminishing (*separating*); the orb will be increased to exactness (*partile*) or decreased out of relevance. Because of the importance of the Sun and the Moon, the lights are always regarded as *sending* aspects. The Sun's average daily motion of fifty-nine minutes and eight seconds is faster than the daily motion of Mars, Jupiter, Saturn, Uranus, Neptune, and Pluto. In aspect with these planets, the Sun *makes* the aspect; its

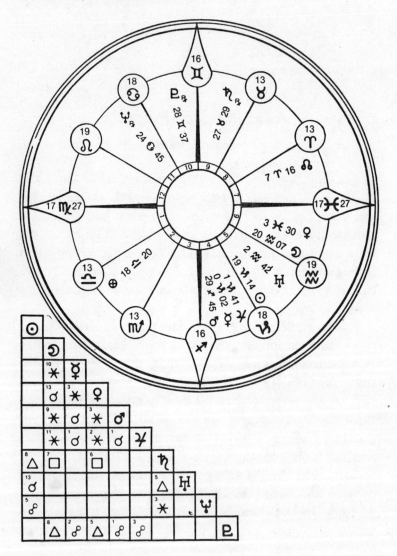

Example 11: Richard M. Nixon
January 9, 1913; 9:44 PM, PST
Yorba Linda, CA; 118 W — 33 N

speed determines the application or separation of the aspect.

For example: the Sun in President Nixon's horoscope is in trine to Saturn with an orb of eight degrees; the Sun, moving faster than Saturn, will gain on Saturn, will diminish the orb of the trine between them. During the lifetime, this aspect will increase strongly, develop within the time of maturation. Additionally, the Sun applies to the opposition with Neptune.

Mercury and Venus move more swiftly than the Sun, having an average daily motion range of one degree and six minutes to one degree and forty minutes and one degree and two minutes to one degree and twenty-two minutes respectively. However, Mercury is never more than twenty-eight degrees away from the Sun, and Venus is never more than forty-eight degrees away: only the conjunction is possible with the Sun.

The Moon moves most swiftly of all the bodies: thirteen degrees daily on the average. The Moon creates aspects with all the other bodies. In an aspect with the Sun, the Moon takes on the active, changeable dimension of the relationship because of its speed and symbolic representation of the changing personality and the shifting events in experience.

In Nixon's horoscope, the Moon is applying to a square with Saturn: during life and experience, the seven-degree orb will be diminished and the promise of the aspect will be dramatically fulfilled. Similarly, the Moon applies to the trine with Pluto, the sextile with Mars, Mercury, and Jupiter. —With such an emphasis upon applying aspects in this horoscope, the awareness of potential is heightened; the unfolding of time and space factors, maturation and development, begins to speak.

Mercury will apply to or separate from all the other planets: in Nixon's horoscope, it applies to the conjunction with Jupiter and the sextile with Venus. —Additionally, note that Mercury separates from the conjunction with Mars and the opposition with Pluto. The separating aspect promises that the significance of the aspect at birth will diminish in life time and development. Applying aspects will take prominence over separating aspects.

Venus will apply to or separate from Mars, Jupiter, Saturn, Uranus, Neptune, and Pluto. In Nixon's horoscope: Venus separates from the sextiles with Mars and Jupiter, the square with Saturn, and the trine with Pluto.

Mars moves a little more than thirty minutes average daily. Mars applies to or separates from Jupiter, Saturn, Uranus, Neptune, and Pluto. In Nixon's horoscope: Mars is *not* applying to a conjunction with Mercury; Mercury is separating; Mars *is* applying to the conjunction with Jupiter; Mars is separating from the opposition with Pluto.

Jupiter moves about twelve to fourteen minutes daily, about two-and-a-half degrees per month, one Sign per year. Jupiter will apply to or separate from Saturn, Uranus, Neptune, and Pluto. In our example, Jupiter separates from the opposition with Pluto; the Moon, Mercury, and Mars *apply* to Jupiter.

Saturn moves about one degree per month, spending

two-and-a-half years in each Sign. Saturn applies to or separates from Uranus, Neptune, and Pluto. In Nixon's horoscope, Saturn can be said to be applying to a trine with Uranus. The retrogradation offsets this (described below).

The trans-Saturnian planets move very slowly: Uranus, about four-and-a-half degrees per year, seven years per Sign; Neptune, about two degrees per year, fourteen years per Sign; Pluto, about one-and-a-half degrees per year, twenty to twenty-one years per Sign.

Retrogradation emphasizes the application or separation of aspects: the applying opposition between the Sun and Neptune in Nixon's horoscope would be *emphasized* by Neptune's retrograde motion. The Sun will gain on Neptune while Neptune will retreat to meet the Sun. The opposition in this case is called a *double-approaching* opposition. —Similarly, the trine from the Moon to Pluto would be a double-approaching trine because of Pluto's retrogradation; the square from the Moon to retrograde Saturn would be a double-approaching square; there is a double-approaching trine between the Sun and Saturn.

The trine between Saturn and Uranus is weak because of the five-degree orb *over the Sign line,* although Saturn appears to apply to Uranus. Saturn's retrogradation symbolically takes Saturn away from this application. Although the tendency is there, the fulfillment will be delayed or weak at best.

Similarly, the sextile between Saturn and Neptune is complicated by retrogradation. Symbolically, one cannot expect easy or swift fulfillment.

The oppositions with Pluto are all separation aspects. The separation dimension is emphasized by Pluto's retrogradation. —In analysis, as we have seen in Volumes III, IV, and V, this opposition axis in Nixon's horoscope is very powerful, involving the only planets in Angles. With our close inspection of the aspects now, we become aware that the difficult opposition significance between Mercury and Pluto—alteration of perspective—would diminish rapidly in the life and *be replaced by the application of Mars to the conjunction with Jupiter,* all out of the way of Pluto. Still, the birth imprint of the opposition would remain but not as prominently; the growing identity would separate from this emphasis. An overcompensatory or substitution development would take place. In Nixon's chart, at an early age, the X-IV axis would refer to the homelife. We will see in later analysis that the departure of this opposition axis from Pluto corresponded exactly to the Nixon family's change of home when he was very young, to his projection of himself into a grand perspective even at an early age, and to the culmination of his university studies in law.

The application and separation of aspects is important to introduce *an awareness of potential movement, development, and change in time. The imprint of the radix is permanent. Only the promise contained within the radix will be fulfilled through movements in time and space.*

In review: the promise of Nixon's horoscope is a dual profession (Gemini Midheaven) involving law (Saturn in IX; House IV group and the applications to Jupiter, ruler of Sagittarius natural to IX, placed on IV) and public, patriotic service (Pluto axis and placement in X; Capricorn Sun; Neptune ruling VII placed in XI and opposed by the Sun); the realization of tremendous ambition (Moon square Saturn, trine Pluto), emphasizing foreign affairs and international ethics (Saturn in IX). The whole horoscope would work to fulfill needs for unusual humanitarian service (Moon in Aquarius in VI, ruler of Cancer on XI). The emphasis upon applying aspects made by the Sun and the Moon stresses the ambition factors. The tendency to introversion and the developed analytical, feeling function (northwest quadrant; Volumes IV and V) combine with the Virgo Ascendant to promise reserve, mastery of detail, and a certain coldness and practicality in the style of self-fulfillment.

Now, in the study of prediction, of movement and development as a function of horoscopic time and space, we must be able to prepare an answer to "When will the parts of the whole unfold?" For example: it will be extremely important to decide *when* the very difficult double-approaching opposition between the Sun and Neptune will gain highest focus in the life development. This is a major threat to development through self-delusion or delusion by friends and a loss of goal orientation. Regarding Moon-Saturn, we should be able to see *when* the ambition potentials will be in highest focus. —The radix system is intriguingly simple: using the Sun, Moon,

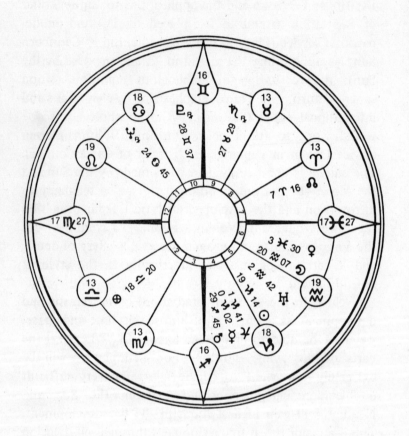

Midheaven, and Ascendant as significators and projecting them according to the equation one degree equals one year to get an approximate time of highest focus, we can begin to approximate the answers to time questions.

Nixon was elected to the Senate on 7 November 1950. He was thirty-seven years and ten months old. If we add thirty-seven degrees (one Sign plus seven degrees) to the Sun at nineteen Capricorn, the Sun is *progressed* to twenty-six Aquarius, *applying to the square with Saturn, the trine with Pluto, and the sextile with Mars!* The Sun would be in House VI just past the Moon. The developmental tension (square) of Nixon's ambition would be dramatically charged in humanitarian service (Aquarius, VI), projected to the public professionally (Pluto in X). —If we add thirty-seven degrees to the Midheaven at sixteen Gemini, it is progressed to twenty-three Cancer, applying to the conjunction with Neptune. One year later, at exact conjunction, Nixon was involved with controversy over a secret fund raised for him by friendly businessmen. Adding thirty-seven degrees to the Ascendant at seventeen Virgo, the Ascendant is progressed to twenty-four Libra in House II, personal finances, exactly square the "difficult" Neptune! The radix system is astoundingly accurate here in portraying tremendous public development of personal ambitions and professional difficulty through friends, delusion, and personal finances ... the development promised by the birth horoscope.

The Sun and Moon radix progressions (sometimes called *directions*) involve the "public," western hemisphere in Nixon's horoscope; the Midheaven and Ascendant

Primary Directions

Years	Degrees	Minutes		Months	Minutes
1	0	59		1	5
2	1	58		2	10
3	2	57		3	15
4	3	57		4	20
5	4	56		5	25
6	5	55		6	30
7	6	54		7	35
8	7	53		8	39
9	8	52		9	44
10	9	51		10	49
20	19	43		11	54
30	29	34		12	59
40	39	26			
50	49	17			
60	59	8			

Calculations

☉   19 ♑ 14   ☽   20 ♒ 07
      +27   02   +27   02
       46 ♑ 16 or 16 ♒ 16   47 ♒ 09 or 17 ♓ 09

MH   16 ♊   ASC. 17 ♍ 27
      +27   +27   02
       43 ♊ or 13 ♋   44 ♍ 29 or 14 ♎ 29

⊕   18 ♎ 20
      +27   02
       45 ♎ 22 or 15 ♏ 22

progressions involve the personal, egocentric eastern hemisphere. —In his thirty-seventh year, Nixon entered national politics as a Senator. His personality "went public." At the same time, a stigma was attached to his image, to his personal dealings, that will endure throughout his public career.

Nixon was elected president on 5 November 1968 at age fifty-five years and ten months. He assumed office eleven days after his fifty-sixth birthday. Adding fifty-six degrees (a sextile minus four degrees) to the Sun at nineteen Capricorn progresses the Sun to fifteen Pisces, applying to the conjunction with seventh cusp! Reelection four years later progresses the Sun to the exact sextile with its own birth position; the Moon progresses square to the Sun, applying to the square with Neptune as well (no calculation necessary: simply progress the significators a sextile for sixty years). Here was life fulfillment indeed, but the Sun-Neptune birth potential for delusion was again strongly activated. The second presidential term would see the application of progressed Moon to square with radical Neptune. The Moon would be in House VIII: other people's resources.

The radix method has received many attempts at refinements, most notably by Sepharial, the British astrologer who wrote textbooks in the first two decades of this century. [1] In 1918, in his book *The Science of*

---

1. Sepharial's real name was W. G. Old. Nineteenth-century astrologers took occult names, names of angels of the Zodiac to create a transcendental atmosphere about predictive Astrology and to protect personal identity from legal prosecution against Astrology. There were many Raphaels; a Mercurius Herschel; R. J. Morrison became Zadkiel; W. F. Allen became Alan Leo. —See *Urania's Children* by Ellic Howe for a fascinating review of Astrology's modern history in England, Germany, and the United States.

Foreknowledge, Sepharial submitted what he called "the most consistent and fully-tried system as yet published." He used an increment of arc—a constant interval of progression—equal to fifty-nine minutes and eight seconds per year, the Sun's actual mean daily motion, instead of the approximate one degree. He added this increment to the Sun, Moon, Midheaven, Ascendant, and Part of Fortune and then studied the progressed aspects made by these five significators to the promissors—the planets—*that remained in their birth positions.*

In a second operation, Sepharial added the same increment for the age being studied to all the planets (*not* to the Sun, Moon, Midheaven, Ascendant, or Part of Fortune) and then studied the progressed aspects made by these planets to the five major significators that remained in their birth positions. —Sepharial called these two operations *primary directions.*

At a glance, the table on the top of page 34 computes the increment of primary arcs for any age. Applying the refined method to Nixon's chart for his marriage on 21 June 1940, at age twenty-seven years and five months, we use the arc 27 degrees and 2 minutes: (19 degrees and 43 minutes for twenty years) plus (6 degrees and 54 minutes for seven years) plus (25 minutes for five months). Added to the birth positions of the five major significators, the progressed positions are as indicated in the calculations on the bottom of page 34.

The aspects made by these progressed significators to the planets remaining at their birth positions are as follows:

☉ applying to conjunction with the radical Moon (four-degree orb)
exactly trine the radical Midheaven
trine to the radical Part of Fortune (two-degree orb)

☽ exactly conjunct the seventh cusp
separating from a square with the radical Midheaven
applying to sextile with the radical Sun (two-degree orb)

MH applying to trine with the seventh cusp (four-degree orb)
applying to opposition with the radical Sun (six-degree orb)

ASC applying to a square with the radical Sun (five-degree orb)
applying to a conjunction with the radical Part of Fortune (four-degree orb)

⊕ applying to sextile with the radical Sun (four-degree orb)
applying to trine with the seventh cusp (two-degree orb)

The only exact (partile) aspects formed are between the Sun and the radical Midheaven (trine), suggesting personal honor; and the Moon conjunct the seventh cusp

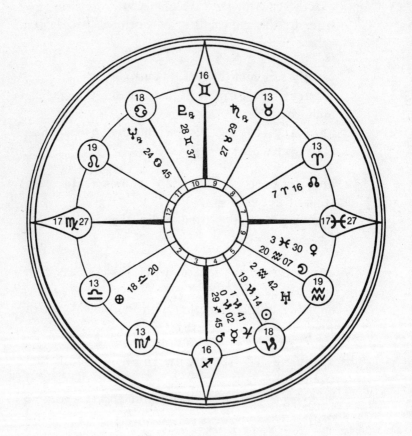

(Angle) of the House of marriage. Together, these are strong indications of marriage. —The progressed applying aspects are positive, promising completion between two and six degrees into the future. The first table on page 34 converts the additional arc of four degrees (the midpoint of this future period, for approximation) to a time just short of five years, five years after his marriage, early in 1945. *The potentials of the birth horoscope* promise public service, law, government. The applying progressed aspects are positive, involving all the major significators, perhaps culminating with the awareness opposition between progressed Midheaven and radical Sun, profession and life-energy, rewards for professional speculation (six-degree orb, just six years). —This was the time period when Nixon prepared his plan to run for Congress, culminating six years after his marriage with his first election to the House of Representatives.

Sepharial's second step was to add the same arc to the planets. The progressed positions and aspects are as follows:[2]

♂ 26 ♑ 47, applying to trine the radical Saturn (one-degree orb)

☿ 27 ♑ 03, exact trine the radical Saturn

♃ 28 ♑ 42, departing from the trine with the radical Saturn

♄ 29 ♒ 44, exact sextile radical Mars, departing trine with radical Pluto

2. Modern practice applies the arc to all radix positions, not just to the prime significators (see page 47).

♀ 00 ♈ 32, exact square to radical Mercury from
House VII

♄ 24 ♊ 31, applying conjunction with radical Pluto
(four-degree orb)

♇ 25 ♋ 39, departing conjunction with radical
Neptune

♆ 21 ♌ 47, opposition with radical Moon, applying
to square radical Saturn

We see the powerful progressed development of Mars,
Mercury, and Jupiter in trine with the radical Saturn,
indications of extreme ambition, expressed well. The exact
trine from Mercury (ruler of the Ascendant) suggests that
the entire Self is clear about objectives, that older advisors
(Saturn) are helping Nixon even at the time of his
marriage. His wife is involved in the development plans
through the square to radical Mercury from progressed
Venus in VII. Additionally, the departing trine between
progressed Jupiter and radical Saturn corroborates the fact
that studies of law were completed, that Nixon was ready
for opportunity and challenge to ambition. The applying
trine from progressed Mars to radical Saturn promised the
energy for further development, the major development
promised by the applying progressed Saturn radical Pluto
conjunction, four-degree orb, nearly five years into the
future.

The opposition between progressed Neptune and the
radical Moon and this Neptune's progressed square to
radical Saturn suggested "camouflaged" problems ahead as
well.

These progressed aspects are interpreted in terms of the potentials promised by the birth horoscope; the birth present is reflected in every present that follows. This is vitally important. —The suggestion that Nixon's wife was significantly involved in the grand plan of his ambition's fulfillment (the progressed Venus exact square to Nixon's Ascendant ruler, Mercury, at the time of their marriage) is definitely rooted in the potential of his birth horoscope: Neptune rules Pisces on the cusp of VII, the House of his wife. Neptune is in XI, love-received and goals, in double-approaching awareness opposition with Nixon's Sun. Venus is exalted in Pisces and is in the Sign of Pisces in House VI (helpers) in the birth horoscope, and Mrs. Nixon is herself a Pisces. Through the progressed aspects, the marriage "present" was expanded out of the birth present, the seed of potentials.

Sepharial devised a *secondary directions* part to his radix system. He took the average daily motion of the Moon, thirteen degrees and ten minutes, equated it to one year, determined the arc for a given age to the birthday month, and then subdivided the given year into months at one degree and six minutes per month. This was an internal refinement that, in his hands, supported the deductions of his primary directions. The table on page 42 makes computation of the secondary arc quite easy. For Nixon at twenty-seven years and five months of age, the calculations are as indicated under that table. The progressed Moon had returned precisely to its own birth position at Nixon's marriage. This in itself would not signify marriage; progression of the Moon in this system

☽ Secondary Directions

Years	Signs	Degrees	Minutes	Months	Degrees	Minutes
1	0	13	11	1	1	6
2	0	26	21	2	2	12
3	1	9	32	3	3	18
4	1	22	42	4	4	24
5	2	5	53	5	5	29
6	2	19	3	6	6	35
7	3	2	14	7	7	41
8	3	15	25	8	8	47
9	3	28	35	9	9	53
10	4	11	46	10	10	59
20	8	23	32	11	12	5
30	1	5	18	12	13	11
40	5	17	4			
50	9	28	50			
60	2	10	36			

Calculations

Completed

☽ Signs	Degrees	Minutes	
10	20	07	Radical Moon, 20 ♒ 07
+8	23	32	arc for 20 years
+3	2	14	arc for 7 years
+0	5	29	arc for five months, to June, 1940
21	50	82	
or 21	51	22	(minutes to degrees)
or 22	21	22	(degrees to Signs)
or 10	21	22	(one cycle of Signs subtracted; −12)

Progressed Moon position for June 1940: 21 ♒ 22 (21°22′ more than ten completed Signs, through Capricorn).

would always return the Moon to its radical position in any horoscope at age twenty-seven through twenty-eight. But the progressed Moon in the primary directions was *precisely conjunct the seventh cusp,* definitely connoting marriage in a man's horoscope (the progressed Sun is the indicator in a woman's horoscope), a suggestion reinforced by the progressed Sun trine with the radical Midheaven. The secondary direction supported further and emphasized Nixon's personality and his needs through the woman in his life (the Moon, House VII).

The refinements that have been made and used in different ways by many prominent astrologers over the centuries do give a keener accuracy to prediction. The approximation can be made at a glance, i.e., by equating one degree with one year, and then the refinement fifty-nine minutes and eight seconds for one year can be made when the first approximation indicates a situation of potential relevance. The secondary operation can further focus monthly progress within the primary prediction year. Analysis of the progressed relationships is then made *in relation to the potentials discovered through initial analysis of the birth present.*

Yet—as intriguingly valid as the radix system appears—it must be stated that the premise is simply not astronomically sound. The planets projected by arcs determined by the motion/time equation have no reference to the motions and positions of the planets at the future moment after birth. Man assumes that the motion/time equation is valid, based upon his rotation on the Earth axis once each day and his orbit around the Sun once each year. But linking this relationship to planetary positions projected into the future defies actual fact.

Since we calculate the birth horoscope meticulously, a slight error in the horoscope can upset the calculations of any prediction system. The birth time must be accurately determined or rectified. How can it be that we abandon exact portraiture of the heavens when we devise systems to project into the future ... and yet, they often *do* predict accurately?

Perhaps all radix and Secondary Progression systems are wrong and the correct system has yet to be discovered; success may be coincidental. Or perhaps there is another answer to help explain the dilemma, made possible in modern time, by modern knowledge and metaphysical formulation.

Time is not absolute. The theory of relativity states that time and space are different aspects of the same reality, that *time is a property of the "world" in which it is measured. Each individual has his own time awareness, his own development space.*

The horoscope in its wholeness is man's own individual time awareness, his own developmental space. In it are included time flow and growth potential. Presents, pasts, and futures are all included. The horoscope is a seed of time, to grow and bloom with the individual Sun.

The meticulously calculated horoscope of the birth moment establishes a highly intricate system of interrelationships that, *in its integral completeness of human creation, transcends actual time and motion.* When man is born, he gains possession of a horoscope; he takes on an imprint from the heavens that is total; he becomes a complicated subsystem of the whole, existing *in its own time and development space.* The horoscope becomes his personal, archetypal entity. This subsystem fulfills itself in the person's *own* time and space.

The interrelationships among the planets in the horoscope gain age through solar orbit and experience through Earth rotation. In one year, with reference to the Sun, the human subsystem is exposed to the life energy of a year's rotation through the Zodiac. In one day, with reference to the Earth, that system is exposed to the experience development of one day's rotation within the Zodiac. All the while, the internal, interrelated system—the birth horoscope taken out of actual time—evolves in a scheme of development promised at birth, completely personalized in experience, and conditioned by the external position in yearly orbit and daily rotation. Individual man develops at his own pace. —Through and within his horoscope, man possesses his own system, his own time to become.

Astrology's different prediction systems are the lines of deduction that make tangents to the system's circle, the horoscope. Enough lines, enough tangents, and the whole is illuminated.

In line with this hypothesis, it is not surprising that one system of prediction seems to apply with better results to a given horoscope than another system. The highly individualized time and space equation within the personal horoscope that has been taken out of *actual* time may respond better to one astrological prediction approximation (tangent) than to another.

It is not surprising that individual astrologers find themselves using one prediction system more satisfyingly than another: astrologers identify more with one system than another through experience in using the system to explain their own Astrological thinking and awareness. —The system applies to the astrologer as well as to the individual horoscope!

Thus, as the student may be informed, so must he be cautioned: the radix progressions in Nixon's horoscope are extremely dramatic. But there are horoscopes in which radix progressions simply do not seem to apply, except perhaps for those of the Sun and Midheaven. In these other cases, Secondary Progression will apply (Chapter 4) and transits will be exceptionally important (Volume VII). Parts of different systems may come together to capture somehow the personalized time-space measure of the individual horoscope. —The few radix observations in Nixon's horoscope are not the only significations of these dramatic events in his life. There were powerful transits operative and strong Secondary Progressions in the background. Different lines of measurement and reasoning worked together to reveal the development of the potentials in Nixon's horoscope. The radix methods give an awareness of their structure and developmental time scheme.

It is not unusual for horoscopes of the famous to respond best to Astrology's systems: highly specialized, public figures seem to fulfill horoscope potentials more than the average person. Their horoscope lives are public record; more details are available for corroboration. The horoscope of a public figure seems to respond more closely to actual time and development expectation.

Rapport measurements. Basically, radix systems define a *rapport,* a sympathy of reference between bodies within the horoscope. In his *Astrology of Personality,* Dane Rudhyar called these measurements of interplanetary sympathies (developmental relationships) rapport measurements. He treated these measurements less formally, as a general indication of development potential, applying the same equation of one year equals one degree to all planets, not separating primary and secondary increments, formal significators and promissors, as Sepharial had done.[3]

For example: in Nixon's horoscope, Uranus and Mars are separated by thirty-three degrees. This is a semi-sextile aspect (thirty degrees) with a 3-degree orb. It is not a major aspect, but is is an indication of the inclination to fulfillment between these two planets. The rapport measurement between them would be thirty-three years.

—Uranus is trined by Saturn (weakly). Mars in IV here is identified with Nixon's patriotism, his energy applied for his homeland. Uranus is strong in its own Sign, Aquarius,

3. Sepharial was inconsistent about separating the major significators from the promissors in measuring his primary directions aspects. There is a definite blend from primary directions into rapport measurements. The most important considerations are the development and constancy of the arc. For approximation, an aspect from any progressed body to any radical position is relevant.

and gains dignity through the Sun's wide applying conjunction. Uranus rules VI here and will definitely represent Nixon's individuality in unusual, humanitarian service.

Rapport measurement establishes that Mars came to Uranus in thirty-three degrees (thirty-three years). Contemplating a career in politics, young Nixon was elected to the House of Representatives in 1946 at thirty-three. The plan was undoubtedly conceived earlier when he was in the Navy in 1942 through 1946, perhaps for the two years when Jupiter, then Mercury joined *Uranus* through rapport measurement. Venus by rapport measurement of thirty-three degrees (years) joined the North Node, an indication of particularly good fortune with the public (VII), a taking in of the public experience.

Rapport measurements are essentially the same as radix directions. But the term *rapport* perhaps describes better the real use of these measurements: to become aware of potential.

An astrologer particularly adept with radix approximations would see the simple progression and rapport measurements very quickly. Then, he would check through other lines of prediction theory: transits and Secondary Progressions, for example. Through various lines of approximation, he would "zero in" upon the potentials stated in the birth horoscope, guided by the corroborations of actual experience. On Nixon's election day in 1968, the astrologer would have noted Saturn's rapport with Neptune: fifty-seven degrees. Nixon was then almost fifty-six. Deceptions and frustrations—promised by the birth horoscope (Sun opposing Neptune)—would possibly be highly focused a short while later. A tremendous fulfillment of international ambitions would also be expected—promised by Saturn's position in the birth horoscope.

But these deductions would only be approximations. More thorough study would suggest a delayed reaction (perhaps the retrogradation factor of Saturn and Neptune) to hold back the crisis until the environment (transits) pressed and Nixon's developmental inclinations responded (Secondary Progressions), perhaps until Fall 1974 and Summer 1975.

Throughout his analysis, the astrologer would inspect different "presents." He would first inquire about a change of home at an early age, when the Midheaven progressed into the X-IV opposition axis; he would ask about marriage at twenty-seven, a powerful individual speculation at thirty-three, great achievement at thirty-seven, and a grand public fulfillment at age fifty-five through fifty-six. The different presents would grow out of the potentials shown in the birth chart, revealed by the applications of aspects and the movements after birth indicated by radix directions and rapport measurements—movements in tune somehow with the horoscope's own personalized time and space continuum. *The horoscope would come to life in approximation.*

Further measurements and reasoning would refine deductions. Time and development structures would begin to form through awareness of potential.

The factor of 7. The maximum strength of an aspect is focused when the aspect is exact, partile. Orbs extend to a maximum of fourteen degrees for the Sun and Moon and to seven degrees for the planets. Radix rapport measurements can grasp the time development to partile through the applying planet and the time development out of focus through the separating planet and diminishing orb of its aspect. Major aspect development can be projected through shifting the radical application of one planet *to* another with which there is no birth-horoscope aspect-orb, or into an aspect relationship different that the one taken on at birth.

For example: in Nixon's horoscopé, Mars was not in conjunction orb with Uranus at birth but was significantly projected to the conjunction at thirty-three years (degrees); Saturn and Neptune are in weak sextile at birth but were significantly projected to the conjunction at fifty-seven years (degrees).

Nixon's Moon is in double-approaching square with Saturn. This is an extremely powerful aspect, promising extraordinary drive and ambition as we know, especially significant since Saturn is ruler of the Sun-Sign and is highly elevated. By the radix rapport measurement, the developmental relationship between the Moon and Saturn in square would be exact at seven years and then fade. But this is certainly not the case. —The sextile rapport with

Saturn (Moon progressed to 27 Pisces) would occur at thirty-seven years (election to Senate, 7 November 1950); the semi-sextile, thirty years later at sixty-seven; the conjunction at ninty-seven.

Of course, the progressed sextile rapport would carry the potential of the birth square relationship into the new supportive relationship of the sextile. But the lifetime is dedicated to fulfillment of the whole, to highest focus of the potentials of the birth imprint *symbolized by development of partile aspects.* Perhaps there is a special time and development factor within the application and separation of aspects, based not upon one year of life, but *upon a greater archetypal time factor that may apply significantly to larger time and development measures.* Perhaps another lens can expand the birth-present significantly.

To the ancients, numbers were holy, the number seven especially. "Seven" weaves itself through history, custom, legend, language, and astronomy with tremendous frequency and ubiquity. Here is a quotation from the *Westminster Dictionary of the Bible* that reveals much about this fascinating number:

> Seven is an ordinary numeral, and it was commonly used without religious significance; but it was also a sacred number among the Hebrews and other Semites, and of Greece. Its sacredness is traceable to remote antiquity. It is seen in the 7 pillars of wisdom's house (Prov. 9:1), the 7 locks into which Samson, who was consecrated to God, braided his

hair (Judges 16:13, 19), the 7 victims to atone for the broken covenant (II Samuel 21:6, 9), the 7 stones of the ancient Arabs smeared with the blood of the covenanting parties (Herod, iii, 8), the 7 lambs to attest the conclusion of a treaty (Gen. 21:28-30), the Hebrew words for oath and taking an oath, which incorporate the number 7, and the sacredness of the 7th portion of time. It was held sacred because men believed that God recognized the number. He placed 7 luminaries in the sky: Sun, Moon, and 5 planets. The Moon has its phases every 7 days. These phenomena, however, were but confirmatory and served as reminders of a greater recognition. God had blessed the 7th day and hallowed it. Seven did become a sacred number, and the 7th portion of time a sacred season; and not merely was the recurring 7th portion of time sacred, but it involved a benediction. It was cherished in hoary antiquity as a season of divine favor toward man, when the manifestation of God's good will was to be expected. (Philadelphia: Westminster Press), p. 546.

"The 7th portion of time ... a benediction ... a season of divine favor toward man, when the manifestation of God's good will was to be expected." Haunting words. Perhaps the portion of time linked with seven can suggest the favor of completion through partile aspect, the fulfillment of horoscopic potential.

Even today, our language contains sayings of superficial meaning but very deep reference: "seven years bad luck," "the seven-year itch," "lucky seven." In Teutonic legend, the flying Dutchman returns to shore every seven years to redeem, to perfect his fate.

Before the discovery of Uranus (1781), Neptune (1846), and Pluto (1930), Saturn was the end of the line, so to speak, the final planet in the system, whose orbit of twenty-eight to thirty years was the length of the average life span in earlier times. Saturn was the symbol of Kronos, time itself. The quadrature (quartering, "squaring") of Saturn's orbit in transit around the Sun corresponded to powerful experiential times in life ... and still does: at seven a child is given a first push toward independence, out of the home and into school; at fourteen, the adolescent is face to face with his own times, and puberty confirms the onset of adulthood; at twenty-one, the young adult, out of college, able to vote, marry and be independent, is welcomed into society; at twenty-eight, he or she makes decisions with experience and maturity, usually changing the way or level of life definitively as Saturn returns (in transit) to its birth position in the horoscope. The second orbit continues with similar meanings at quadrature: a fresh push to independence at thirty-five, "second" adolescence at forty-two, and development toward retirement around fifty-six to sixty. The increment of seven is dramatic. —The original Sabbath, the seventh day, was Saturn's day (Saturday). Saturn in the horoscope is the major symbol of developmental time and experience. Saturn's orbit prescribes man's architecture of advance as he meets his environment (fully studied in Volume VII).

In primary directions, one degree of the Zodiac rising

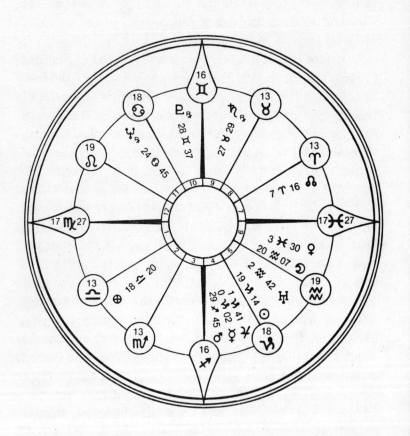

above the horizon in four minutes of time gains an equivalence to one year of life. Twenty-eight minutes of time would represent seven degrees or the measure for seven years of life experience. The lunation cycle is twenty-eight days/years with quadrature points (phases) of seven days/years each. —Additionally, in the astrological House system, House I-to-VII polarities make the dynamically meaningful opposition axes throughout the horoscope.

Perhaps we can bring all the lore of "7"—the structure of the lunation cycle and its phases, Saturn's orbit and its quadrature points, and the formalized social emergence of the individual—to the study of aspect completion in the birth horoscope. The factor of "7" may be a portion of time that "divinely" favors man's fulfillment. —*By assigning the factor of seven years to every degree a birth aspect has receded from or advanced toward completion, we can often deduce a time scheme of the maturity and emergence of this aspect in life.* Perhaps the measurement of application to partile indicates a rise in prominence of the aspect within the life; perhaps a measurement of the separation orb indicates a strong statement of the aspect at some point within the life and a diminishing of relevance thereafter.

For example: in Nixon's horoscope, we see immediately that Mars makes a double-separating opposition to Pluto from House IV. The nature of the aspect suggests that it would be highly focused soon in the life and then diminish in relevance. The effect at that time would certainly involve the home, a relocation or upset

(Gemini; Mars, Sagittarius) through the parents (X, IV). Mars and Pluto are separated by 1 degree and 8 minutes or just eight years. —The double separating opposition Mercury-Pluto involves 1 degree and 24 minutes or approximately a little more than 1 1/3 degrees (24/60ths),which gives a time span of a little over nine years (1 1/3 or 4/3 times 7 years equals 9 plus years). The development to be expected would be travel, study, an intensification of Self (Mercury rules the Ascendant), and perhaps a precocious awareness of profession (Pluto in X). —The double separating opposition between Jupiter and Pluto would suggest education success, maybe extended travel, home removal, and awareness of public opportunity. Jupiter and Pluto are separated by 3 degrees and 3 minutes, a little over 21 years using the factor of 7 years per degree.

When nine years old, Nixon did move from Yorba Linda to Whittier, California, a University town. Much has been written of how he would lie awake at such a young age and dream of getting out and getting ahead and of how he received honors in college. —The factor-7 time scan corroborates actual development.

The Sun is making a crucially important double approaching opposition with Neptune. The promise is for delusion by friends (XI) or self-delusion, public speculation about personal goals (XI is the fifth of VII). In Cardinal Signs, the emphasis of this aspect can be expected to be within action, within active development. By the factor-7 time scan measurement, the highest focus of this applying aspect would be at thirty-eight years (5 degrees and 31 minutes or 5½-degree orb; 11/2 times 7 equals 38 plus), the period in 1951 and 1952 when Nixon was caught in controversy over a secret fund raised by friendly businessmen. Additionally, we must recall that the primary direction of the Midheaven conjoins Neptune also at thirty-eight and the direction of the Ascendant squares this Neptune at thirty-eight from House II. —This key opposition-point in Nixon's life saw the birth of the perennial "tricky Dick" epithet.

The Moon's double-approaching square with Saturn —extremely powerful in any horoscope—promises a driving potency in work, administration, service; a powerfully structured ambition (Taurus) projected into foreign affairs (House IX). By the factor-7 measurement, the difference between the Moon and the exact partile position is 7 degrees and 22 minutes or 7 1/3 degrees, giving a time of a little less than 52 years, when Nixon began his comeback drive in 1965. He had lost the election for president in 1960 and the California election for governor in 1962. In 1965, a "new Nixon" appeared campaigning hard for Republican Congressional candidates for the election in 1966. —Then, at the same time, the Sun completed the double approaching trine with Saturn, indicated at birth: 8 degrees and 15 minutes or 8¼ degrees times 7 years equals 57 years plus, almost 58 ... 1971, the height of Nixon's popularity, when he made history by visiting China and Russia as president. The entire horoscope was fulfilled by time-system development between the Sun and the Sun-Sign ruler, promised in the birth horoscope.

Throughout development, the Capricorn personality factors (Sun) would establish the nature and mode of development. Those factors are eloquently described by the press in countless references to Nixon's "persistence, durability, ambition, tactical shrewdness, his stress on order, 'holding himself in his own iron grip', his sobriety, stamina and control, his 'making one thing perfectly clear'." With reelection in 1972, news analyses of Nixon's strategy and campaigning platform continued to reveal the tremendous scope of his projection (axis X-IV), his posture (Sun-Neptune), and potency (Moon-Saturn)—all of which cloaked Capricorn: "in terms of style, Mr. Nixon stressed order, which he thought he could impose, rather than charisma which he knew he couldn't project. His ambition, he once said, was to restore 'respect' to the presidency"; the phrase "historic first" proved to be his favorite; his most prominent achievements occurred in the field of foreign affairs, which Mr. Nixon has long considered his "strong suit"; he had to end the Vietnam war on an "honorable basis"; his values were the traditional ones of the work ethic, law and order, national security. —The entire horoscope speaks. Only the Neptune-Sun opposition remains hidden from full view.

Quick examination of the horoscope in terms of radix progressions (rapport measurements) and factor-7 time-scan has revealed all these potentials and the general schedule of their accentuation and unfolding. We have worked with the birth present and expanded it to new presents. Arcs of projection promised in the birth chart have been projected and corroborated within time; experience has confirmed analysis and supports further projection.

The factor-7 measurement works—as often and as reliably as other systems. But it too is astronomically unsound, having nothing to do with actual planetary movements in time and space. Yet, somehow it can be in tune with the horoscope's own personalized time and space continuum expressed through individual development: "the 7th portion of time."

Factor-7 Table

Degrees of orb	Years	Minutes of orb	Years	Months
1	7	1		1+
2	14	2		3−
3	21	3		4+
4	28	4		6−
5	35	5		7+
6	42	6		9−
7	49	7		10+
8	56	8		11−
9	63	9		12+
10	70	10 (1/6°)	1	2
11	77	20 (1/3°)	2	4
12	84	30 (1/2°)	3	6
13	91	40 (2/3°)	4	8
14	98	50 (5/6°)	5	10

The projected arc of prediction. Let us imagine that President Nixon visited an astrologer in 1963, the year after he lost the California election.

The astrologer would draw the horoscope, analyze the basic configurations easily. He would test several radix observations about the change of home as a child, the graduation from college, law study, marriage. The expanded presents would cover election to the House of Representatives, the Senate, the vice-presidency, and the period of losses. Nixon would want to know what was going to happen to him.

The astrologer would probably concentrate on the fulfillment of the Moon-Saturn square (due through factor-7 measurement in 1965), the rise of the progressed Sun to the seventh cusp due near 1970, and the fulfillment of the Sun-Saturn trine (due through factor-7 measurement in 1971). He would check many more measurements, especially transits. He would sense a "gathering of forces" in Nixon's horoscopic time and development process. He would question Nixon's plans and learn of a possibility to start again through a Congressional campaign in 1965, two years into the future. Then he would discuss the potentials with Nixon, being extremely aware of Nixon's focus of ambition and the need for fulfillment.

He would be able to project a tremendous new wave of ambition, seasoned through experience, achieving lifetime goals in the specific years ahead.

He would also note extremely carefully the maturation of the Sun-Neptune opposition: activated by radix directions of the Midheaven and Ascendant at 37 years of age, this axis corresponded to accusations of fraudulent management of funds and misplaced trust in associates. —At the same time that the progressed Sun would sextile its own position having just crossed the seventh cusp in Nixon's sixtieth year in 1973, the Moon's one-degree-equals-one-year rapport projection would place it square the Sun-Neptune axis. What had happened in the past at thirty-seven would probably be activated again at sixty, in 1973!

The astrologer could make a prediction; the projected arc would have gathered enough substance in the past to justify a powerful, seemingly "impossible" prediction for the future. Nixon would be riding high at that time but again would be open to speculation about fraudulent dealings and scandal.

The prediction could have been made for this occurrence when Nixon was thirty-seven or long before then. But it would have had less substance since the Sun-Neptune axis had not yet been fully activated. In the prediction for age sixty, the astrologer has the substance of corroboration through the incidents at thirty-seven.

The student is not yet fully prepared to understand the fine measurements that would justify this prediction completely. These will be covered in Volumes VII and VIII. However, this analysis is a perfect illustration of how the astrologer builds his awareness of potential, substantiates his awareness with corroborative experiences, and frames his prediction accordingly. Many measurements play a role; the whole gradually reveals itself.

4

Development of Potentials
Secondary Progressions

At the beginning of the eighteenth century, there was a shift in the time equation, variously attributed to Kepler, the Arabs, or other researchers, a shift from a concentration upon the radix, from the equation one degree equals one year, to experimentation with a new equation: one day after birth equals one year of life. Instead of one degree's rising over the Ascendant (four minutes of time) being equated to the one-year orbit around the Sun, the exact *whole* unit of one day's Earth-orbit progress after birth was equated to the *whole* unit of *annual* Earth orbit. This was the first progression predictive system that employed time and space after birth—but again, there is no sound reference to actual planetary positions in actual future time after birth (beyond one actual day).

Researchers with these Secondary Progressions found apparent confirmations of their hypothesis in the Old Testament of the Bible: Daniel 7:25, in the hand of God everything is "a time and times and the dividing of time"; Psalm 90:4, "For a thousand years in thy sight are but as yesterday when it is past, or as a watch in the night"; then, Psalms 77:5, "I consider the days of old, I remember the years long ago."

In Secondary Progressions, the planets progress *at their own individual rates.* The movement relativity factor among the planets, established in the heavens and in the birth horoscope, is maintained in Secondary Progressions.

At a glance, Nixon's natal horoscope on page 54 shows a zonal movement potential up to the seventh cusp; picture the Zenith-Nadir axis as the spine of the newborn, the XI-V axis as his out-stretched arms; the "right arm," here the Sun, Uranus, and Moon, will rise, "scooping up" the experience potentials of Capricorn and Aquarius, Houses V and VI, coming to a square relationship with Saturn and trine with Pluto, then to the horizon of awareness, into the House of full public presentation, VII. —Secondary Progressions try to capture this zonal development potential through the *relative* changes of planetary positions after birth.

The calculations are extremely easy: a number of *days* equal to the number of years of projection is counted forward in the Ephemeris after the day of the birth, and a horoscope *at the birth time and place* upon the progressed day is constructed. Nixon was born on 9 January 1913 at 9:44 PM, PST, in Yorba Linda, California, 118 West and 33 North. To inspect the year of his graduation from Whittier College in 1934 at age twenty-one, for example, we simply count ahead twenty-one days from the birth date in the Ephemeris to January 30 (9 plus 21) and construct a progressed horoscope for 30 January 1913, at

9:44 PM, PST, in Yorba Linda, California, 118 West and 33 North. To inspect the year of his marriage at twenty-seven, we would find the progressed birth date by adding twenty-seven days (years) to January 9, the birth date, bringing us to 5 February 1913 (twenty-two days remain in January, plus five more into the next month).

The example horoscope shows the progressed horoscope for Nixon's election to the Senate in his thirty-seventh year (7 November 1950). The Secondary Progression date is 15 February 1913. The horoscope is constructed for the same time and place of birth.

At first glance, remembering the birth chart relationships, what changes have taken place by the time Nixon was thirty-seven years old? The Sun has progressed into *square* relationship with Saturn (an applying trine in the birth horoscope); Mercury, the ruler of the birth Ascendant, is separating from a conjunction with the progressed Sun and a square with Saturn; both make a progressed trine to progressed Pluto. The progressed Moon is applying to a conjunction with the progressed Pluto and an exact trine to the progressed Ascendant. The progressed Mars is in exact trine with progressed Saturn. Progressed Neptune is in double-approaching conjunction with the progressed Midheaven.

Nixon's entire being was charged with the tremendous ambition promised in the birth horoscope through Saturn. His life-energy—his whole Self, his mind—was in powerful developmental tension to fulfill his ambition. His personality needs (Moon) were highly elevated in station, applying to a fulfillment of his

Richard M. Nixon
Secondary Progression Horoscope, 37th year
Birth Date: January 9, 1913
Progression Date: February 15, 1913

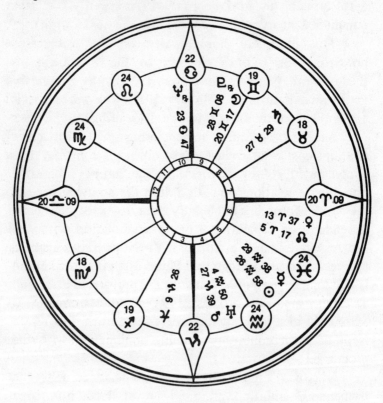

projected professional image. The trine relationship between Mars and Saturn promised that the tremendous energies would work out smoothly and attract the attention of someone older (Saturn). Nixon's energy (patriotism) would be well received through someone else's resources (progressed Saturn in the VIII). —Additionally, the Moon-Pluto and the Midheaven-Neptune relationships suggested something undercover, camouflaged in the profession. The strong square between progressed Sun-Mercury and radical Saturn suggested a powerful thrust of insight. In combination, the energy could very well be synthesized as "detection activity" in the name of patriotism to fulfill political ambition ... especially for a lawyer (the law of naturalness, Volume IV).

In 1950, Nixon was elected to the Senate and led the Senate investigation hearings into the Alger Hiss case, international espionage and political subversion in the United States. He was selected to be Eisenhower's running mate and was elected as vice president two years later. At the same time, he was accused of the "secret fund."—The progressed horoscope speaks clearly to corroborate the record of Nixon's thirty-seventh year.

The progressed positions must be related to the radix positions, to the potentials shown at birth. The most efficient way to picture the whole is to place the progressed planets *around the birth horoscope*. Then, relationships between progressed and radix planets, among the progressed planets themselves, and between the planets and zonal (House) development can all be seen at a glance.

The example on page 68 shows Nixon's radix with

Richard M. Nixon
Radix-Progressed Horoscope, 37th year

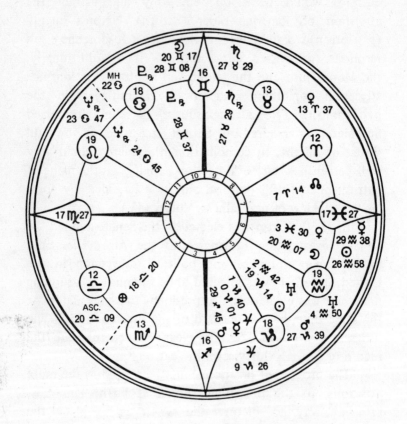

the progressed positions noted as well, both in the same horoscope chart. It is in this portrait that the significances of the thirty-seventh year are perfectly clear:

P.☉♂p.☿□r.♄,△♇   From House VI to IX and X: tremendous developmental tension requiring fulfillment of ambition for public service, involving ethics, law, foreign affairs—all promised by the birth horoscope and accentuated in this 37th year.

P.☽♂r.MH,r.♇,△r.☽,⊕;□Asc.The personality form has "risen" to its highest point, a tremendous focus of career projection and professional perspective; personal worth accentuated; the Self under high tension to succeed.

P.♂△r.♄,♂r.♅;p.☿⚹r.♂Energy flows into ambition easily, "closing in" (applying) on powerful fulfillment of individual service goals (progressed Mars applying to a conjunction with Uranus). Progressed Mercury, ruler of the radical Ascendant, is in excellent, supportive sextile with the radical Mars in Sagittarius.

The entire picture is one of extreme developmental ambition, at its highest point, fulfilling the tremendous personal projection of public service seen in the birth horoscope. —Again, it is clear that the critical Neptune position is coming into high emphasis as the progressed Midheaven approaches Neptune's radical position.

The Moon's Secondary Progression. Similar to Sepharial's secondary directions in the radix method—the monthly subdivision of the Moon's motion—there is a way to subdivide the secondary progressed year into months as well: the Moon's average daily (yearly) motion is thirteen degrees, close enough to twelve degrees for reliable approximation, congruent with the measure of twelve months in one year. In reading the months during the ensuing progressed year, we simply progress the Moon *one degree per month further.* If the Moon is traveling very fast upon the progressed date (noted automatically in construction of the progressed horoscope)—fifteen degrees, for example—then the astrologer keeps this in mind; the progressed Moon will cover a little less than one degree per month. *This measurement of the Moon's progressed position is the most powerful contribution of Secondary Progressions to prediction technique.*

The progressed horoscope always represents the progressed year *beginning with the birthday month.* For Nixon, this is very clear: he was born in January, the first month of the year. The progressed thirty-seventh year begins in his birthday month, in January. The progressed Moon position in the progressed chart represents the position of the Moon in January of his thirty-seventh year, January 1950. —If Nixon had been born in October, for example, the progressed year would begin in October, the birth month, in any given year of life, and the Moon's position would be for October of the given year with successive months added to the first month of the birthday year, October.

Look at the position of the progressed Moon at 20 Gemini. Eight degrees "later," the Moon would come to a conjunction with Pluto; and still one month further, to an opposition with Mars. For the Moon only, eight degrees represents eight months. Since the daily motion upon the progressed date was more then twelve degrees (thirteen degrees and forty-two minutes from noon on the 15th to noon on the 16th), this time period of eight months (Pluto) and nine months (opposition Mars) would be a bit longer, close to 9 to 9½ months after January, to October and November of 1950, Nixon's thirty-seventh year. The potentials of the birth horoscope and the significance of the progressed horoscope for this thirty-seventh year would be highly focused then through the Moon's powerful progressed position: in the Midheaven, upon the dramatic professional axis. —Nixon's election to the Senate occurred on 7 November 1950!

Additionally, with no further computations, we can check the immediate past before this 37th year: twenty-three degrees before the progressed birth date position at thirty-seven, the Moon had been in conjunction with Saturn. Twenty-three degrees equals twenty-three months, close to 2 years. Nixon's progressed Moon was conjunct his radical Saturn two years earlier when he was thirty-five—a tremendous accent of ambition once again: Nixon was reelected to the House of Representatives at thirty-five. —Twenty-four degrees (months) earlier still, at thirty-three, the progressed Moon (3 Taurus) had been square Uranus, a progressed aspect that represents a powerful, decisive new start, a development of strong individuation. Nixon was thirty-three and was elected to the House of Representatives for the first time: speculation about a grand political career is suggested by Uranus in V. (Recall that, through rapport measurements, Mars came to a conjunction with Uranus at thirty-three as well!)

Looking *ahead* from Nixon's thirty-seventh progressed birth date, the Moon would come to a conjunction with the critical Neptune thirty-four months later, three years. The application of the progressed conjunction coincided with the fund-fraud accusations when he was thirty-nine and forty.

In his sixtieth year, 1973, Nixon's progressed Moon is at 16 Aries 30; in April 1973, square the Sun (opposed Neptune in the radix); in September 1973, exactly square the critical Neptune. —Make a prediction!

These measurements of the monthly subdivision are highly dramatic. They complete the progressed picture. These dramatic results are *not* unusual! Through examples that follow in this volume and throughout all your experience in Astrology, the Moon's position within Secondary Progressions will be seen to have extreme importance.

Additional observations. Because of the very slow daily motion of Saturn, Uranus, Neptune, and Pluto, the positions of these planets, measured through Secondary Progressions, vary only very slightly during a lifetime. Their positions and significances in the *radix* have a powerful, enduring symbolism that is keyed by the aspect applications to them of other planets in faster progression and development.

In Nixon's progressed chart for the thirty-seventh year, we see that Saturn is exactly at its birth position, 27 Taurus 29. It appears that Saturn has not moved—progressed—at all. But note: the progressed Saturn is *no longer retrograde*. A check in the Ephemeris reveals that Saturn, retrograde at birth, *assumed direct motion* on 29 January 1913 at 27 Taurus 10; i.e., it assumed direct motion during Nixon's twenty-first year, 1934, when he graduated from Whittier College and planned to enter law school.

We know that a change from retrogradation to direct motion suggests a change or abandonment of counterpoint (Volume IV). With Saturn, the assumption of direct motion suggests a freely focused ambition, a direct application or conception of ambition's direction. Nixon's political speculations were planned at that time and during his service years, 1942 through 1946.

The fact that Saturn had returned precisely to its birth position in Nixon's thirty-seventh year—and then progressed onward toward the Midheaven—is another keen corroboration of this very important, ambitious time in his life.[1]

The student should always carefully note these changes between retrograde and direct motion in progressions. Mercury, Venus, or Mars changing from one motion to another will correspond to strong developments

1. Saturn progresses too slowly to reach Nixon's Midheaven during his lifetime. But the image to keep in mind is of Saturn's going *higher* in life position.

in the life experience, especially when, at the moment of change (*stationary*), the planet makes a valid aspect to a radical planet. A radical Mercury-retrograde in House X assuming direct motion when the native is thirty-two, for example, square to Saturn during the year of change, could suggest a tremendous change of mind about the direction of ambition, perhaps going into business for one's self, depending on the entire configuration. With Venus, the reference would be to the emotions; with Mars, to the energy: an engagement could be broken off when Venus turns retrograde; a child's speech problems may be overcome when Mars assumes direct motion in the natal House III (always depending upon the synthesis of the birth horoscope, of course).

There is almost an exact congruence between the Sun's position by radix direction (one degree or fifty-nine minutes and eight seconds per year) and by Secondary Progression. This is simply because the radix systems are based upon the unit of one degree, the approximate orbit distance traveled by the Earth around the Sun in one day. The Secondary Progressions system uses the Sun's apparent motion (actually Earth motion) in one day which does approximate one degree on the average. A further congruence between the systems applies to the progression of the Midheaven. The progressed Sun and Midheaven are always the same distance apart as the radical Sun and Midheaven. The distance between the two is constant, established in the birth horoscope. Their progressions can be determined at a glance, indicating through progressed aspects the special years for further, more detailed study.

Simply add the age, any age to both the Midheaven and Sun for their progressed position approximations.

Drawing a horoscope for a progressed year really covers *several* years within the same picture. The eye can check the immediate past and the immediate future before and after the illustrated year. One need not draw new horoscopes for every single year within a decade, for example. A single horoscope will suffice: the student can then approximate further movements *from the Ephemeris alone,* timing quite accurately the major conjunctions and aspects anticipated from studying the chart.

Additionally, upon familiarity with the system of Secondary Progression, the Moon's progressed relationship with Saturn—so very important as we shall see—can be calculated throughout a lifetime without even referring to the Ephemeris! Take the Moon's average daily (yearly) motion as twelve degrees and count ahead in degrees in the horoscope to the first square, conjunction, or opposition with Saturn in the birth horoscope. Then, divide by twelve; the quotient is *the age at which the cycle begins.* This relationship between the progressed Moon and the radical Saturn—or any other planet!—will then repeat itself in quadrature (square, opposition, square, conjunction, square, etc.) every six-and-a-half to seven years (the Moon's phase-quadrature in orbit, six-and-a-half to seven days). The increment of six-and-a-half to seven years is successively added to the age at which the cycle begins, and the years of highest developmental tension in terms of the planet can be determined during the lifetime.

For example, in Nixon's horoscope, the distance to

Moon square Saturn is only seven degrees, not easily divisible by twelve. Anyone born with a close Moon-Saturn square (or any other planet) will begin the progressed cycle relationship between these two planets at birth. Automatically, we can project points of focused ambition in the life starting the cycle at birth:

Years of Age	Aspect	Event
6½-7	conjunction	
13-14	square	
19½-21	opposition	
26-28	square	college graduation (21)
32½-35	conjunction	marriage (27)
39-42	square	two terms in Congress (33,35)
45½-49	opposition	elected vice president (39)
52-56	square	lost presidential election (47)
58½-63	conjunction	elected president (55)
65-70	square	reelected president (59)

If the Moon were at 7 Aries (where the Moon's North Node is), the distance to conjunction would be fifty degrees. Divided by twelve: four plus. In this case, we would have begun the cycle at four years of age, adding the increment successively throughout the lifetime: eleven, eighteen, twenty-five, thirty-two, etc.

This approximation measurement with Saturn brings the personality and its needs into *phase* with ambition and its characteristics. Throughout your studies, this progressed aspect relationship between the Moon and

Saturn especially will be very important. The increment of seven, once the cycle is begun, is an extremely swift way of approximating the progressed position of the Moon in relation to Saturn or to any other planet to guide more detailed computation, should a highly significant time be anticipated.

Let us apply this abbreviated approximation technique to a quadrature cycle between the Moon and Neptune. Knowing the critical position of Neptune, ruler of Pisces on VII, in opposition with the Sun, we can anticipate in the life an accentuation of speculation about public administrative service, his appearance to the public (Pisces on VII), and an overtone of difficulty, camouflage, and frustration at various times: the distance between the Moon and the first square position to Neptune (24 Aries) is sixty-four degrees; divided by twelve, the quotient becomes five, the age at which the quadrature cycle between the progressed Moon and Neptune would begin. The approximate high points of relationship focus would be at five, twelve, nineteen, twenty-six, thirty-three, forty, forty-seven, fifty-four, sixty-one, etc. These could be times when Nixon would feel the need to master the deluding side of his personality and ambition ... or the times when he would be easily duped, deceived by others. At ages twenty-five and twenty-six, the progressed Moon opposed Neptune (and, in the same general time period, conjoined the Sun!): marriage was Nixon's chief focus. At age thirty-three he first speculated about a political career and gained his first term in Congress; age forty (conjunction) saw the end of the scandal period; at forty-seven plus he lost the presidential election; at fifty-four he experienced a successful presidential campaign and election; at sixty-one can he expect further tension?

Note that in this approximation technique of the Moon's progressed motion, a specific aspect *will repeat itself in about twenty-eight years* (the Moon's orbit equals twenty-eight days).

With practice, use of approximation techniques becomes second nature. When the systems are fully understood,

- the eye makes radix progressions of the Sun and Midheaven, discovers an important focus;
- applies a rapport measurement that might confirm the discovery;
- applies the factor-7 technique for further approximation and corroboration;
- approximates the Moon progressions in relation to Saturn or another important planet;
- finds one or several years that are indicated by several measurements;
- then creates a detailed Secondary Progression horoscope for careful measurement and analysis.

The initial approximation process usually requires no more than a few minutes; often, important years of focus are spotted in thirty seconds! —And, of course, when a person asks to have his horoscope done, the progressions are focused upon *the present age*. Then, approximation techniques disclose the development in the immediate past and future.

Progressed lunation development. In our study of the development of aspects in Volume III of this series, we began with the focus-blend of two planets at conjunction and the gradual separation of the faster body from the slower one into different aspect relationships. This was illustrated by the movement of the Moon away from conjunction with the Sun. In the phases of the Moon, we see the phases of sunlight reflected from the Moon, measuring the aspect between the two bodies. The New Moon (conjunction) symbolically represents "new light"; the Full Moon (opposition) symbolically represents "full light". In the applications to these aspects, the Moon gains light toward opposition and loses light towards conjunction.

In the symbolism of Secondary Progressions, the lunation cycle is extremely important. In progression, the Sun symbolically brings the statement of horoscope life-energy forward into new zones of experience and into new energy relationships with the parts of the whole. Progressively embellished levels of illumination are achieved through Secondary Progressions. —In progression, the Moon symbolically brings the personality form and receptor of experience forward into new zones and relationships as well. The greater relative speed of the Moon corresponds to the many changes, *development cycles,* and personality adjustments made in life's progress.

Symbolically in the radix and in progressions as well, the Sun and Moon work together; the Sun depends on the Moon for reflection and the Moon depends on the Sun for its own light and energy. When the progressed New Moon occurs—the conjunction between the progressed Moon and the progressed Sun—there can be expected in the life a significant time of "illumination," new direction; the six-and-a-half to seven years before will often suggest a feeling of losing light, of listlessness, a feeling of unimportance relieved by new seeding at New Moon.

When the progressed Full Moon occurs—the opposition between the progressed Moon and the progressed Sun—there can be expected in the life a significant "recognition," "seeing the light"—or the light's being seen; the six-and-a-half to seven years before will often suggest a feeling of gaining illumination, of growth, of importance, of building self-constructs, fulfilled in full-light reflection.

At the top of every month's page in the Ephemeris, the New Moon and Full Moon of that month are listed in longitude degree (and, in later Ephemerides, in Greenwich Mean Time). Of course, a horoscope drawn completely for a progressed date upon which a New Moon or Full Moon occurs will show the aspect relationship immediately, but the lunation polarities can be seen in reliable approximation simply by looking at the Ephemeris page.

In Nixon's birth month, January 1913, the New Moon occurred on January 7 at 16 Capricorn 36 and the Full Moon occurred on January 22 at 1 Leo 53. Looking at Nixon's progressed radix horoscope (page 68), we see that the New Moon occurred two days *before* Nixon's birth and doesn't concern us now.[2] The Full Moon occurred on the thirteenth day after Nixon's birth: the significance of the progressed Full Moon would be seen in Nixon's thirteenth year.

The progressed Full Moon occurred conjunct (Sun) and opposed (Moon) the radical Uranus. In an adult, this would be a very powerful recognition of individuality. For the young Nixon, it was surely a precocious illumination of the "speculation" of his life: law, public service. We can believe the publicity stories about his early day-dreaming about a tremendous career. Additionally, the position of the progressed Full Moon in V (the progressed Sun's position) would emphasize an interest in sports (House V)—the interest the president has to this day.

In February 1913, the New Moon occurred on February 6 at 17 Aquarius 7, approximately in Nixon's twenty-seventh to twenty-eighth year, conjunct his radical Moon, trine the radical Midheaven and the Part of Fortune. Nixon found "new light" through his marriage at that time, a partner with whom to build his dreams of public service, a new seeding of light to grow in the years ahead. —The student surely recalls the radix directions corroborating marriage, emphasizing the Moon (pages 37 through 40).

In February 1913, the Full Moon occurred on February 21 at 2 Virgo 16, approximately in Nixon's forty-third year, conjunct (Sun) and opposed (Moon) the radical Venus in VI, sextile Mars, Mercury, and Jupiter in

2. In Volume XI, the New Moon *previous* to birth is studied for its occult, reincarnation significance.

IV. Nixon gained complete recognition through his reelection as vice president in 1956. This was the high point of his patriotic service, a fulfillment of his political career. —He did not win another election until 1968, twelve years later.

The next lunation cycle began with the progressed New Moon in his fifty-eighth year (progressed date: 8 March 1913) in 17 Pisces 19, exactly conjunct the seventh cusp, sextile the natal Sun. It was in 1971 and 1972 that Nixon's ambitions were illuminated again in terms of the foreign relations and public service dimensions promised by the horoscope. The "new Nixon," newly elected president, journeyed to China and Russia and made history. The coup opened a whole new era in international diplomacy; paved the way for a fresh approach to ending the Vietnam war. The public servant had risen above the horizon, out into the open, his rise complete.

Between conjunction (New Moon) and opposition (Full Moon), there are, of course, points of sextile, square, and trine relationships. The square is the most significant in Secondary Progressions: it occurs at six-and-a-half to seven years, between conjunction and opposition, between opposition and conjunction. The first-quarter phase after New Moon sees a building upon the inspiration of the New Moon period, a utilization of things past taken in new directions. The second-quarter phase, leading six-and-a-half to seven years later to opposition and Full Moon, sees a "construction" period, a breakaway from the past, an initiative to accumulate success and recognition.

The third-quarter phase lasting six-and-a-half to seven

years after the recognition the Full-Moon period sees a dissemination period, a sharing of the light. The last-quarter phase, leading six-and-a-half to seven years later to conjunction and New Moon, sees a waning period, a time of search for new inspiration.

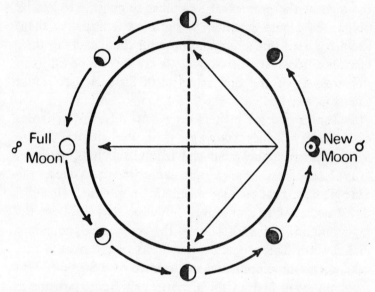

Indeed, in the study of the *radix*, the relative positions of the Sun and the Moon *at birth* reveal much about the personality in terms of the lunation cycle as well. For example, Nixon is born shortly after New Moon; his life will have the first-quarter phase significance always in the background. The emergence of the lunation cycle *within progressions* accentuates whole-development in phases of time and experience.

Analysis of the progressed horoscope must be made in relation to the birth horoscope. The aspects by progressed planets to radix planets are the more important indices of development. The progressed Sun shows the stage of overall self-development at the progressed time: the Sign of the progressed Sun must be considered and its progressed House position *in the birth horoscope;* then, the progressed Sun's relationship with the planets in their birth positions. The measurements are superimposed upon the analysis of the Sun in its birth Sign, House, House rulership, and birth aspects.

The progressed planets show how different activities and identity values cooperate with the progressing life force: Mercury, the mind and mental faculties, attitude, travel, nerves, change and adjustment; Venus, the emotional reactions, aesthetic responses, financial investment; Mars, initiative, impulse, sex; Jupiter, the higher mind, the enthusiasms, the scope of opportunity and reward. The progressed positions of the planets may take on the developmental significance of a Sign different from the birth Sign of the planet, a new House position in progression, different from the birth House position, and certainly new aspects to the other planets in their birth positions. —The progressed nature, position, and relationships of the planets are analyzed *in relation to, upon, as an extension of their significance in the birth horoscope.*

The progressed positions of Saturn, Uranus, Neptune, and Pluto will vary only slightly: ambition, individuation, vision and "camouflage," and public perspective and grand change potential have a great constancy in the life through the birth configuration. The expression of these values is achieved through the other progressed planets applying to new aspects with them.

The progressed Moon develops the most swiftly, giving the personality development many opportunities for change and adjustment through concrete events and assimilated experience.

After the progressed positions are understood as an extension of the birth horoscope, as an expansion within time and space into a new present, the internal aspects of the progressed horoscope can be evaluated: the aspects made by progressed planets with other progressed planets.

The synthesis process is accomplished much more quickly than it can be explained: the horoscope portrait speaks thousands of words. The astrologer *sees* development. At a glance, he learns to see the dramatic development anticipated from the birth horoscope. The planets in movement become animated, become expressive figures in an unfolding drama.

The birth horoscope develops its own scenario, its own unfolding of potential, its own scheme of time and space. It is responsive to its own internal order, its own integral inclination to complete itself. The astrologer's systems illuminate the different lines of development in different ways: radix methods reveal "degrees" of change; the factor-7 system may define the larger scenes and highpoints within the drama's acts; Secondary Progressions reveal the role of the actors—all following the intentions of the playwright known from the beginning. Together, the whole is continuously approximated, finely enough to allow knowledgeable evaluation and appreciation.

5

Interpretation of Progressed Aspects

In the first five volumes of this series, we have studied the symbolic meanings of the planets and their aspects without reference to time. With the introduction of time and development, the substance of the meanings does not change, but the meanings are adapted to the development process. For example, the Sun symbolizes life-energy, the nature and mode of life-illumination. In progressions, this core meaning must be adjusted to the process of becoming illuminated. So, the key meaning for the progressing Sun is "illuminating." The adjusted meanings of the planets illustrate the developmental dimension of the planets' basic meanings:

☉ illuminating
☽ experiencing
☿ moving, learning, worrying
♀ loving, socializing, financing
♂ energizing, accelerating, disrupting
♃ expanding, legalizing, inheriting

87

Saturn and the outer planets retain their basic meanings as well. But, as *receivers* of progressed aspects from the inner planets, they relate dimensions of becoming to distinct spectra of development:

ħ   ambition; structural development
♅   individuation; change and separation
♆   vision; spiritual development
♇   perspective; grand alteration

These slight changes help in articulating analysis of the progressed horoscope: as the progressed Sun comes to major aspect with a radical planet, it illuminates, "bestows" an illuminating dimension upon the radical planet. The analysis then synthesizes the *condition* of the Sun in the birth horoscope, i.e., its Sign, House position, and aspects, the condition *that is brought forward* by the Sun in progression—its birth meaning, *with the condition of the radical planet receiving the progressed* "illuminating" aspect.

The whole process is one of unfolding, of change and development, of reorganizatition—*but always in terms of the potential promised in the birth horoscope* seen through the birth-horoscope condition of the progressing planet.

☉ The Sun ☉

Sun-Mercury
The easiest progression to measure and understand is that of the Sun. Almost invariably, when the Sun

progresses to a conjunction with Mercury (by radix direction at one degree or fifty-nine minutes and eight seconds per year or by exact Secondary Progression), Mercury's meaning in the birth horoscope will be illuminated, will receive the illuminating emphasis of the progressed Sun: an accentuation of studying, learning, writing, expression, perhaps moving, traveling, possibly an accentuation of the nervous system. —The interpretation would bring together the birth condition of the Sun and the birth condition of Mercury *through* the developmental condition of the Sun in its progressed position.

For example: if the birth horoscope showed Mercury in Aries in VI, opposing Uranus in Libra in XII, the astrologer would immediately study the potential of a highly geared nervous system, a nervous anxiety that could cause sickness (VI, XII). The Sun could be in Pisces, behind Mercury, in V. Perhaps there would be a Scorpio Ascendant. Add to this picture a Mars in VIII square the Sun—noting that this Mars would rule Aries on VI and co-rule Scorpio on the Ascendant. The horoscope would look like the one on page 90.

The configuration is highly emphasized through the mutual reception of Mercury and Mars, and the square in *Mutable* Signs between the Sun and Mars. The Sun in progression *will bring with it* the significances of this birth square with Mars: high nervous reactions, possibly causing sickness.

Scanning quickly, we can see that the progressed Sun would join the radical Mercury in fourteen degrees, approximately fourteen years. At that time, we could expect the potential nervous condition to be highly illuminated, emphasized. The Sun's progressed conjunction with Mercury would not really help matters, since the Sun has the Mars-square imprint at birth. The condition would be aggravated, probably beginning four years earlier when the progressed Sun would oppose the radical Uranus. —This is seen in a flash!

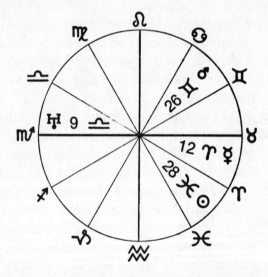

We could then make a very quick check of the Sun-Mars square: the Sun is separating from exact square, two degrees out of partile at birth. By the factor-7 measurement, the two degrees are translated into an approximation of fourteen years. —a corroboration! Again, this process would take only a matter of seconds.

Additionally, by rapport measurement, adding fourteen degrees (years) to the Mars position progresses

Mars to 10 Cancer, square to the birth Uranus *and* the birth Mercury.

These speed approximations indicate an emphasis upon the fourteenth year as the time of crucial development of the potential problem. The astrologer would know immediately that the progressed Moon would be opposite its own birth position (fourteen years, one-half the progressed Moon's cycle). He would check the Moon position quickly. He would rapidly progress the Midheaven, the Ascendant, perhaps Venus (as ruler of Libra on XII). With knowledge of transits (Volume VII), he could check immediately the *actual time* of the fourteenth year.

The fourteenth year immediately would capture the focus of analysis. —Enough approximation would have begun to reveal the whole; further, detailed study would qualify the initial deduction.

An analysis of the problem behind the nervousness would involve understanding the impressionability of the Pisces Sun in V—perhaps adolescent (fourteen years) concerns about love, sex, feelings—corroborated by the Scorpio Ascendant and the prominence of Mars in the configuration. Of course, the position of Neptune would have to be considered as ruler of the Sun Sign and the Sign on the Vth House; the position of Pluto as ruler of the Ascendant; and, most importantly, the position of the Moon in relation to the needs of the personality (Volume V). Saturn's position would show the native's ambition leading his development and perhaps would be significant in describing the native's relationship with brothers and sisters (ruler of Capricorn on III), very important in adolescence. Venus would be important as well—never more than forty-six degrees from the Sun, definitely somewhere in the northwest quadrant. All of these other planets would have *their* "conditions." —*The point here is that the entire horoscope would be focused into the meaning of the potential* suggested by Mercury opposed Uranus, Sun square Mars, illuminated by the progression of the Sun.

In an actual horoscope with Mercury in Capricorn in VIII squaring Mars in V, the Sun at birth placed in VII in excellent conjunction with Jupiter, quite a different manifestation occurred when the Sun progressed to a conjunction with this Mercury at nineteen: the native received a conspicuous honor at his university (Mercury, Jupiter) and, at the same time, made the first long, extended journey of his life (Jupiter, Mercury).

Mercury's square with Mars accentuated keen pursuit of studies—and a nervous developmental tension about learning, communication, discovery. This was emphasized by Mercury in Capricorn in VIII. The Sun brought with it in progression the expanding (educational, traveling) dimension of the Sun-Jupiter birth conjunction. All together, the manifestation in experience was easily expected.

This is the process of synthesizing progressed aspects into developmental meanings. In the suggested aspect-meaning guides in the following pages, the most probable developmental energies are described. The astrologer merges the birth significance of the progressing planet with the promissor planet in its birth position through these specific developmental energies.

P. ☉ ♂ ☿ Dimensions of learning, communicating, worrying, adjusting, moving, traveling are illuminated by the Sun in conjunction.

P. ☉ ⚹ ☿ (A sextile, square, or trine can be made by
 △ the *progressed* Sun and the radical Mercury; never in the *birth* horoscope because of Mercury's nearness to the Sun). There is increased awareness, mental alertness; plans are working well; attitude is constructive.

P. ☉ □ ☿ This progressed square suggests worry, anxiety; possibly leading to travel and diversification; also contract problems, employee tensions, sibling tensions; unsettledness in preparation for change.

Sun-Venus
P. ☉ ♂ ♀ The emotions are illuminated, spotlighted. When this progressed conjunction occurs after fifteen years of age, an intensification of romantic development occurs. At a marriageable age, especially in a male horoscope, marriage is strongly suggested, or an intense emotional bond.

In an artistic horoscope where Venus, Neptune, Libra, Pisces, Leo, and/or Aquarius are very important, this progressed conjunction can suggest a culmination of aesthetic interests.

In a horoscope where Venus is related strongly by position, rulership, or aspect to House II or VIII, to Taurus especially, this progressed conjunction may have much to do with financial focus in the life, investment, luxuries

When the progressed conjunction occurs very early in life, the illumination will probably be in the socialization process or pass unnoticed. At an age after marriage it may suggest a second marriage, an affair, or an intensification of the emotions or financial concerns within the marriage or work.

For example: if the progressed Sun makes a square to the radical Uranus before the progressed conjunction with radical Venus, divorce or separation could well occur, to be followed by a new emotional relationship and/or marriage.

P. ☉ ⚹ ♀ Emotionally, aesthetically, socially, and financially, developments in the life will be beneficially illuminated. A positive time for improvement, expansion, and reward; and for marriage.

P. ☉ □ ♀ This progressed square may lead to unpleasantness with regard to emotions, sociability, finances; usually accompanied by a challenge to improve self-projection, to adjust the energy of relationships.

Sun-Mars
P. ☉ ☌ ♂ A challenge to the developmental system is suggested by this progressed conjunction: energy is highly illuminated. Affairs are accelerated, brought to a climax.

The native becomes temperamental, lacking in self-restraint, extravagant.

In a female horoscope, this progressed conjunction can suggest a very powerful relationship with a man, indicating marriage (similar to progressed Sun conjunct Venus).

Energy is illuminated to develop the potentials shown in the birth horoscope. Mars is a catalyst highly fired by the progressed Sun.

P. ☉ ✶ ♂ These progressed aspects are very favorable
    △   for applying energy to new enterprise. Independence flows well in an active and progressive period.

P. ☉ □ ♂ A very challenging time is indicated by this progressed square. Very frequently, it accompanies surgical operations—as does the progressed Sun square *progressed* Mars. The life-energy is brought into extreme developmental tension with tremendous energy. Much depends upon the condition of health in the birth horoscope to determine how the organism will hold up under such challenge. Plan must displace impulse; health must be guarded. —Anticipating this period can channel the tremendous developmental energy positively into a strategically slowed-down planning of future development. Without anticipation, the life accelerates into a period of duress and collision ... part of the body may give way.

P. ☉ ☍ ♂ In this extremely important progressed opposition, the Sun sends full developmental illumination to the capacity to apply its energy. Grand decisions will have to be made. Under the challenge, health and wisdom must be constantly checked. A time of tremendous dynamic opportunity when anticipated, planned for, and strategically paced.

Sun-Jupiter

P. ☉ ☌ ♃ This progressed conjunction indicates an extremely fine period—if the birth Jupiter is not in debilitated condition in the birth horoscope. Health, education, extended travel, financial success are all indicated. If the birth Jupiter *is* debilitated, the progressed Sun will move into the debilitation as well: then, excesses can be expected; benefits can be wasted.

Of course, in the very young, this progressed conjunction will refer to advantages through parents or education. With maturity, international travel can be indicated if it is promised in the birth horoscope; bonanza, if the birth horoscope promises wealth; publishing opportunities, if the birth horoscope shows writing potential; inheritance, if House VIII conditions are positive.

It is a time of expansiveness, enthusiasm, and opportunity.

P. ☉ ⚹ ♃ Prosperity and success are indicated,
△   especially by the trine.

P. ☉ □ ♃ These progressed aspects point to a period
     ☍   of tendency to excess, to over-doing in
over-confidence. Developmental tensions can present
themselves as obstacles rather than challenges.

When this progressed square or opposition
accompanies indications of romance problems and/or
divorce—impulse, separation, emotional involvements—the
legalism meanings of Jupiter are introduced. Similarly,
should there be a crisis in a professional situation indicated
by other progressed aspects and promised in the birth
chart, legal transactions will surely come into the life's
concern.

In the periods of difficulty, there will always be a
reward potential, a "silver lining." Again, the progressed
square or opposition is not victimization: it is challenge.
Anticipation is warning, and warning is preparation.
Involving Jupiter, the Sun illuminates a period of
opportunity; through the square or opposition, a struggle
will be necessary. —Look for the potential gain from the
difficulty.

Sun-Saturn

P. ☉ ☌ ♄ The aspects with Saturn are infamously
    □   drastic according to older astrological texts.
    ☍   Times were slower and more confined
then: ambition had few ways open for expression and
development. In modern times, ambition is expected;
individuation is demanded; outlets abound.

The progressed Sun relating to Saturn is extremely

important: it is a time *to grow up!* It is a time to come to grips with what the individual life is all about.

Eisenhower changed jobs at Sun Square Saturn: he became Chief of Staff of the Third Army and then Commanding General of the European Theatre. —He was well prepared for the shift: he had been MacArthur's assistant in the Phillipines.

Older texts warn of tremendous upset at these times, jobs and marriages broken up, etc. But one must understand that *change or loss is essential for a new level to be developed.* In older times, maintaining the prescribed status quo was synonymous with fulfillment, good personality, health. In modern times, routine living and expression is not preferred: the spirit of enterprise and material improvement reigns, demanding drive, ambition, adjustment, change, and upset. What threw older horoscopes into disorganization, now can organize the modern horoscope to greater achievement.

Under these progressed aspects, the native who is unprepared, who has not seen his ambition and personality lucidly enough, will easily interpret loss or change as characterological crucifixion! Instead, the native should note personal failing that need adjustment and change for improved advancement. Perhaps the whole developmental system is calling out for fresh application. What are the person's dreams, hopes, needs? An aspect with Saturn brings man into developmental tension with his ambition.

Older texts predict a loss of a loved one. This must happen at certain times in all lives. But life does go on! Abraham Lincoln's mother died when he was ten years old, with Sun square Saturn. But his father remarried the next year: a new period was beginning as one ended.

During these Sun-Saturn periods, a sick person may indeed become sicker: the organism can become depressed when the routine of things is disrupted, feel lost when security is disrupted. But sickness is a call to action, action to repair, mend, rejuvenate. The time measure can indicate when the period will end, when the aspect will separate, when new health and plans will begin to work "uphill."

During these Sun-Saturn periods, one may feel worthless—in terms of past routine, past goals, past expectations. Check Saturn's Sign, House, and aspects in the birth horoscope very carefully. Distill the full nature of personal ambition (see Volume VII). Check the personality's needs through the Moon (Volume V). Study House XI, its Sign, planets, aspects, and ruler. Find ambition's true, mature perspective; the new way out of the challenging period will be discovered. Check the progressed Moon's movement during the period and try to identify the potential experiences ahead. Transits will be very important as well (Volume VII) to show the press and opportunities within the environment.

Sun-Saturn periods crystallize the whole of the personality. Twenty-seven percent of all U.S. Presidents through Nixon were born with the Sun conjunct, square, or opposed Saturn: they carried this tremendous mark of drive and ambition with them throughout their lives! In great part, that is why they became president. —Another twenty-five percent had the Moon conjunct, square, or opposed Saturn!

P. ☉ ⚹ ♄ These progressed aspects to Saturn improve
△   reputation, establish the worth of
ambition's display, invite the helpful attention of elders.
Goals will gain support and solidify in application. —Hitler
was proclaimed Fuehrer under the sextile.

Sun-Uranus

P. ☉ ☌ ♅ The individuation potential marked by
Uranus's condition in the birth horoscope will be
illuminated. Friends, innovation, sudden changes in life,
separations will gain significance for the life development
that follows. —With Saturn and the outer planets, periods
of illumination have long-lasting significances in
life-development thereafter, always in terms promised by
the planets' conditions in the birth horoscope.

P. ☉ ⚹ ♅ These periods almost invariably mark the
△   most fortunate periods of life, the
"luckiest" periods. Individuality flows most smoothly;
friends are helpful, innovation succeeds, the environment
rewards. —Hitler launched World War II with successful
invasions of Poland, France, Belgium, Holland, and
Norway under the trine.

P. ☉ ☐ ♅ This progressed square indicates an
extremely powerful period of developmental tension.
Individuality is stressed; there can be expected a
breakaway from the status quo, sudden
change—geographic, marital, professional, health—in terms
of Uranus in the birth horoscope.

Very frequently, this progressed square with Uranus in a female horoscope corresponds with divorce or separation: the female absorbs enormous tensions for individual assertion, and the marriage usually suffers unless an outlet is found to recognize her individuality more. In a male horoscope, the same tensions occur but are manifested more in the profession.

The periods indicated by this progressed aspect reveal high tension, worry, upset. The system is being challenged; the individual wants to break free.

During these periods, one is best advised to "take stock" rather than fight, to make strategic alteration rather than impulsive change. The duration of the period (about three years) demands *cooperation* rather than blind ego-assertion. —This does not mean that the personality must step aside and disappear for the period. That is impossible under this aspect! Rather, every emotional and egoistic assertion must be strategically tempered, adjusted with knowledge of the tendencies of the period. Enormous *efficiency* of personality expression can be achieved during this progression through careful planning.

P. ☉ ☍ ♅ Much of the square aspect is seen within the opposition, but the stress appears to come from the environment more than from within the individual. It is a time of self-recognition that can be imbalancing for some people. Change, upset, and tension challenge the Self to be, to make adjustments, shift direction, relate differently.

Sun-Neptune

P. ☉ ☌ ♆ Fantasy is illuminated: religiousness, aesthetics, psychic inclinations; delusion, camouflage, substitution. Very much depends upon the condition of Neptune in the birth horoscope. The personality's unconscious is awakened. There is a sensitization to the "soul" of things, perhaps a yearning for the ideal.

At thirty, Hitler's progressed Sun conjoined his radical Neptune in VIII. He became obsessed with the idea of regenerating Germany according to legendary traditions.

P. ☉ ⚹ ♆ These progressed aspects indicate benefits
△ spiritually, artistically, psychically; refined sensualness; uncanny, "unreal!" good fortune.

P. ☉ ☐ ♆ Tremendous, pervasive developmental tension exists in spiritual, psychic, and aesthetic dimensions of life. The tension can be very great, requiring a stabilizing progressed aspect (sextile or trine by a planet with Saturn, for example) or an extraordinarily settled birth horoscope to gain maximum benefit from this intense period.

Charles Manson's Sun squared his exact radical Neptune-Mars conjunction at ages twenty-six through twenty-eight: he tried to become a songwriter and performer in Hollywood, conceived a Messiah image for himself, began taking drugs. His personal rebellion began.

Many researchers link Neptune with "revolution," a substitution of one thing for another; many see Neptune as camouflage, the appearance of something as other than it really is. —The significance of Neptune is vague, and this vagueness is the difficulty especially with the progressed Sun-Neptune square. The sensitive dimensions of the personality are keenly alerted for change (rebellion), for reaction (possible camouflage), for idealization (substitution).

P. ☉ ☍ ♆ This progressed opposition indicates a period of extreme awareness, leading the personality to acute sensitivity. With stabilizing factors in the radical or progressed patterns, great opportunities can be realized. Without stabilizing factors, the life may wander seriously off course.

It is important to note that with Neptune especially—and with Uranus and Pluto—aspects may pass unnoticed in the life of the child, the early time "presents" of a horoscope. If the birth horoscope is powerfully structured around Neptune or if Neptune is ruler of the Sun-Sign or the Ascendant, there may be manifestations at an early age through the parents. If Neptune is involved within sickness structures, meaning that the organism is weakened in the birth present, the progressed conjunction, square, or opposition may indeed aggravate the condition.

The astrologer Alan Leo, some thirty-five years after Neptune was discovered (1846), suggested that "Neptune allows the soul to leave the body." Progressed aspects to Neptune illuminate that which is personally unusual; the formless; the challenge and opportunity of the intangible.

Sun-Pluto

P. ☉ ☌ ♇ Personal perspective within the world is illuminated. The personality experiences motivation to gain recognition or to make deep personal revisions in order to attract it.

P. ☉ ✶ ♇ The personality experiences easy,
△   successful projection of Self into the world. Activity matches expectations.

P. ☉ □ ♇ Personal perspective within the world is under developmental tension. There is the opportunity for personal reformation in this very deep, powerful period of reorganization, ends and new beginnings.

Lyndon Johnson went through this period in his early twenties upon graduation from college when he began to teach school. His plans were made for marriage and for attending law school for a career in state and national politics.

P. ☉ ☍ ♇ This is a very difficult aspect. The environment appears to break up the personal order for new starts, for radical change. —During this opposition, Eddie Rickenbacker, the celebrated aviator, sustained serious injuries in an airplane crash in the United States and then, shortly thereafter, he was forced to ditch an airplane in the Pacific Ocean.

Sun-Sun

P. ☉ ☍ ♇ When the Sun progresses to a sextile with

its own birth position, it is a signification of good health and energy and marks a very successful period should other progressions confirm the potential. Age sixty is a turning point in life.

P. ☉ □ ☉ When the Sun progresses to a square with its own birth position, when the person is just over ninety years of age, it is a time of health consideration.

Sun-Moon

P. ☉ ☌ ☽ The Self's needs and projections are totally illuminated. If other progressions indicate change, this progressed aspect will certainly support the period cynamically. Here, "illumination" is definitely the key word.

P. ☉ ✶ ☽ These progressed aspects are very favorable.
△ The whole Self runs smoothly—a great assistance should difficult progressed aspects among other planets be forming.

P. ☉ ☍ ☽ This progressed opposition indicates change, adjustment; possible difficulty with the health; keen awareness of the action of the will.

Sun-Angles

The four Angles of the horoscope are very important points of change. The Ascendant refers most to the personal health, the projection of the Self; the fourth cusp, the Imum Coeli, refers most to the ends of matters and new beginnings; the seventh cusp, the Descendant, refers to emergence into the public, marriage, relationships, partnerships, etc.; the tenth cusp, the Zenith or Midheaven, refers to personal and professional honor. —Practically in every normal lifetime, the progressed Sun will at some time cross over an Angle. That time in the adult personality will be extremely important, marking a new epoch in the life.

Ascendant:	Calvin Coolidge's progressed Sun came to his Ascendant at fifty-three and fifty-four: he was inaugurated president in his own right, after having completed Harding's term.
Imum Coeli:	Jefferson married an heiress; Garfield was assassinated.
Descendant:	Nixon at fifty-nine and sixty visited China and Russia and was reelected for his final term as President.
Midheaven:	Truman was elected U.S. Senator; Jacqueline Bouvier's engagement to John F. Kennedy was announced.

☽ The Progressed Moon ☾

The progressed Moon will traverse the entire horoscope once every twenty-eight years, making every aspect with every radical planet. Allowing a three-degree (month) application and separation orb, the aspect periods have a duration of about six *months,* most focused at the partile midpoint.

Above all, the meaning of the progressed Moon aspects is found in actual experience. As the Sun's reflector, the symbol of the personality's form in development, and the symbol of the personality's ever-adjusting needs, the Moon "collects" the experiences of development. It marks man's developmental space within his personal time scheme, his phases of maturation.

The progressed Moon spends approximately two years in each radix House (more when a Sign is intercepted in the House). During this House progression, the affairs of the House in the birth horoscope will be emphasized.

Moon-Houses

P. ☽ in I   This period is the time of clearest personality emphasis in development. The enormous alterations in life-expression experienced when the progressed Moon crosses the Ascendant will be stabilized during this period.

P. ☽ in II   All matters of finance and personal worth; the partner's financial condition; and often, aesthetic substance will be accentuated in relation to the changes made when the Moon crossed the Ascendant.

P. ☽ in III   Developments of about five years before (more if there is an interception in I or II) need and gain adjustment. There can be concern, thought, frequent travel in connection with pending change. All things written, communicated, or surmised through critical evaluation come to the foreground. The person begins to look ahead to a new beginning.

P. ☽ in IV Again, the Moon crosses an Angle: a time of special new beginnings; matters come to an end, and a definite new period begins. Affairs of the home, house, residence, and parents; changes of location, sympathy, and emotions; and often a dimension of subtle inspiration can be expected.

If the progressed Moon makes strong aspects with House VIII structures that promise inheritance, this period can often see its manifestation.

Overall, it is usually a favorable time since the Moon has a natural rapport with House IV, ruling Cancer, the Sign natural to it.

P. ☽ in V   The new beginnings made during the period in House IV are solidified, structured in terms of the emotions, children, ripened speculation, creativity, theatricality, and friendships gained through the partner.

P. ☽ in VI This is an especially sensitive zone: if VI in the birth horoscope is configurated negatively, promising poor health, this progressed period may aggravate the situation through the aspects made by the Moon. If VI is positive in the radix, excellent developments can be accumulated in relation to the work situation, job offers, relationships with colleagues, self-criticism, diet, and the economy of the work effort.

P. ☽ in VII Again, the Moon crosses an Angle: a time of fresh emergence into the public, invigorated relationships, rising out of the preparation period that perhaps began seven years earlier when the Moon crossed the fourth cusp.

P. ☽ in VIII The personality's relationships with others may be emphasized by cautious investment, separations or death, inheritance, an awakening of a deep sense about meanings in life.

P. ☽ in IX As the Moon approaches the Midheaven, affairs take a loftier, more expansive path, usually based upon affairs experienced about five years earlier and matured when, just before, the Moon was in VIII. Extended travel, legal experience, philosophical and religious development can be involved. The "foreign experience" can mean not only international experience but mental expansion into new directions as well.

P. ☽ in X Crossing the Midheaven, the Moon corresponds to emphatic changes and adjustments in the profession or in the position of personal honor and self-esteem. The home and perhaps the parents will be affected; a strong time for full achievement, with probable reference to the periods when the Moon crossed the seventh cusp and/or the fourth.

P. ☽ in XI Friendships gained through the preceding

period will be strengthened. The personality will be concerned with its reception by others. New objectives, hopes, wishes will be formulated, surely with the spouse or a very close friend.

P. ☽ in XII The personality is preparing for a new cycle of personal development. The worth of the past cycle is measured and evaluated sensitively. The deeper part of the nature is strongly awakened. Experiences with hospitalization, death, separations, the occult or psychic realm will all affect the personality's adjustment of goals conceived in the preceding period. —There is a feeling of confinement and emptiness, an awaiting of new change and ego rejuvenation.

Each of these House periods becomes remarkably clear in careful study of the radical and progressed horoscope. Progression through each of these zones of development will correspond to new "presents" of experience. —After age twenty-eight, the Moon will begin a new progression cycle within the individual radix; *the same progressed aspects and pattern of development will begin again.* The astrologer gains a tremendous advantage with a horoscope progressed past 28: *he can check experiences manifested in the past cycle to substantiate further his deductions about experiences to be manifested in the future cycle.* Of course, other progressed aspects will be forming at different, much slower rates, and the Sun will be making new, different progressed aspects with the radical planets. But the Moon *will repeat* the tendencies of experiential development based upon an expanded present, a grander pyramid-base of past experience. The manifestations in development wlil be at a different level; the apex formation of prediction beginning higher up the structure.

Because of the Moon's high sensitivity and the speed of its progressed aspect formation, its condition and reference within the *birth horoscope* are especially important. The Moon brings with it not only meanings of the personality's form and its needs, but the experience reference from its position in the radix and the *House that it rules.*

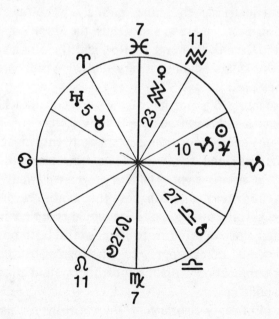

In the portion of an actual horoscope, printed on page   , the progressed Moon in the 28th year "triggered" powerful configurations in the birth horoscope: the conjunction of the Sun and Jupiter in VII emphasizes the public thrust of horoscope life-energy. A public opportunity fulfills this man. This conjunction trines in Taurus in XI. Public appearance and personal projection fulfill the personality's wishes and goals for individuation. Venus and Uranus are in mutual reception, linking these hopes and energies significantly with foreign experience, travel, the arts. The trine between Venus and Mars in House V confirms the creativity dimension. The Moon in Leo adds further confirmation of the personality's needs to be theatrical, to shine publicly. The awareness opposition between Moon and Venus, the Moon's applying trine with Uranus, Sun and Jupiter, and the Moon's exact sextile with Mars establish a very unified synthesis of the horoscope part.

Inspecting this portion of the horoscope quickly for the twenty-eighth year, we note that by factor-7 time scan, the Moon-Venus opposition is exact at twenty-eight years (4-degree orb) and the Venus-Mars trine becomes exact similarly at twenty-eight. The Sun progressed twenty-eight years (degrees) approaches the ninth cusp. —At twenty-eight, the progressed Moon would complete its first progressed cycle and return to its powerful birth position. Then it would quickly apply to the progressed trine with Uranus, conjunction with the fourth cusp, and trine with the Sun and Jupiter.

In his twenty-eighth year, the native won a national

competition as an opera singer and was rewarded with European contracts. This was the culmination of study begun some five years earlier when the Moon had crossed the Ascendant and led to a home relocation to Europe four years later when the Sun entered House IX. A grand new beginning was achieved when the Moon made vital progressed aspects during the twenty-eighth year. The Moon rules Cancer on the radical Ascendant: the native's entire personality was changed, as reflected in his new home and "sympathies," which fulfilled a hope and goal with which he was born. (Note: the Moon is exalted in Taurus holding Uranus.)

Moon-Mercury

P. ☽ ☌ ☿   This progressed conjunction stimulates the experiencing of activity, movement, adaptation, versatility, and communication, in terms of the condition of the Moon and Mercury in the radix.[1] It is associated with creative emotional anxiety, study, detection, criticism, work.

P. ☽ ⚹△ ☿   The mind will work well in reacting to experiences. Opportunity for significant mental development and constructive communication. The native will be heard and listened to.

---

1. Naturally, whenever the Moon makes a progressed *conjunction* with any radical planet, these "conditions" will be easiest to synthesize since the planet's position will have been already understood from birth chart analysis and the progressed Moon will have entered *the same zone*. The Moon's position will be synthesized in the same terms with the additional dimension of the Moon's position and rulership in the radix.

P. ☽ □ ☿ The mental faculties may be anxiously stirred; nerves may be unsettled; concentration, difficult. Misunderstanding may arise.

P. ☽ ☍ ☿ The personality's critical nature will be under tension; motives, difficult to explain. Close personal relationships may be stressed.

Moon-Venus

P. ☽ ☌ ♀ This aspect indicates artisitic inclination, aesthetic experiences; socially, imaginatively, and emotionally, harmony will be experienced. Personality needs are balanced by fulfillment.

P. ☽ ⚹△ ♀ The conjunction, sextile, and trine are excellent support aspects to "heavier," more dramatic aspects (those involving the slower moving planets) under formation at the same time (almost always the case). These are aspects of harmony. With the sextile and trine especially, a broader scope of profitable relationships will be experienced; the harmony extends further out from the Self.

P. ☽ □ ♀ There may be momentary difficulties with interpersonal relationships, emotional, aesthetic, or financial concerns.

P. ☽ ☍ ♀ The opposition brings keenest awareness of Venus's significance in the birth synthesis. Personality and emotions, aesthetics and finances come into sharp awareness. —If there is a progressed square aspect by any planet to Mercury at the same time, criticism may be discharged into emotional relationships.

Moon-Mars

P. ☽ ☌ ♂ The birth-synthesis meanings of Mars are highly exposed in experience. Applied energy will be challenged by experience.

P. ☽ ⚹ ♂ The application of energy will be eased. There is a danger that it may flow too easily, in too great quantity. The potential of Mars is extreme, and the progressed relationship of the Moon invites its full expression in experience: decisive thinking, creative action, sexual expression, working out of ambition.

P. ☽ □ ♂ Developmental tension surrounds the birth-synthesis of the Mars condition. Experience will more often than not jar energies into impulse reactions.

P. ☽ ☍ ♂ This progressed opposition suggests a time of potential disruption and change; there should be a full awareness of Mars potential as shown in the birth horoscope. Resolution of obstacles and problems should be delayed during the passing of this short period.

Moon-Jupiter

P. ☽ ☌ ♃ A very positive aspect, this one encourages expansion through the experiencing of opportunity in terms of Jupiter's condition in the radix. An excellent period for exertion of the personality's resources toward fulfillment of plans.

P. ☽ ⚹ ♃   Opportunities may abound. Legal
     △   arrangements will favor the native. Investment opportunities should be taken advantage of. There may be a strengthening of ethical position through law, religion, or the psychic area.

P. ☽ □ ♃   Usually, this is a period of momentary extravagance, over-exertion, over-eating, over-spending, over-indulgence. By extending personal capital too far, there is the possibility of legal difficulties (especially if Jupiter is squared or opposed at the same time by the progressed Sun, etc.). If the square is related strongly to VI by position, aspect, or rulership, health may be taxed by excesses.

P. ☽ ☍ ♃   A time to economize and efficiently organize rewards and opportunities. New gains will be made through others' losses rather than personal initiative. Awareness of ethical considerations is needed.

Moon-Saturn

P. ☽ ☌ ♄   The progressed Moon's conjunction,
     □   square, and opposition to Saturn are
     ☍   extremely important periods in life-development. The aspects are so powerful that the orb

of application and separation must be studied very carefully, even extended to embrace totally these emphatic periods of development. For example, the personality will definitely be planning strong career activity at these times: allowing a six-degree (six-month) application and a six-degree separation, the whole developmental year can be carefully studied month by month, incorporating other aspects that may be made by the progressed Moon to other planets during the application to and separation from Saturn.

These periods every six-and-a-half to seven years after the cycle begins mark developmental tension between the personality's form and needs and the life-ambition. Experiences press for decision and maturation. These aspects can be best interpreted as developmental *calls to action.*

In the study of transit theory (Volume VII), it will be seen how often the progressed relationship between the Moon and Saturn comes into phase and cyclic rhythm with the transit of Saturn through the horoscope in actual time. Together, these measurements complete the personality's *architecture of advance.*

Older texts again predict disastrous difficulty at these times; caution, resignation, and passivity are advised. But in modern times, ambition has an outlet. Passivity within modern times and modern society *invites* being passed by, being unfulfilled. Staying at home misses opportunity. Neglecting the spirit of adventure weakens the muscles of reaction. —Modern times demand individuation and give opportunity for the development of personal ambition. The progressed Moon's relationship to the radical Saturn marks these periods unerringly.

For the very young during this aspect, change may be realized through the parents, especially the father. For the housewife, it may be very important for her to begin to do "something" during these periods, to start projects within the home or without, to refurbish, change, improve—as suggested by analysis of the birth horoscope. Inactivity may allow the call to action to pass easily; but more often than not, the tensions appear disruptively, seeking outlet in other dimensions of life.

P. ☽ ✶ ♄   Experiences take the flow of ambition
      △   easily to fulfillment. There can be recognition and help from elders. There is a seriousness connected with these positions that will bring thoughtfulness, maturity, and a creative sense of responsibility to the work expressing ambition.

Moon-Uranus

P. ☽ ☌ ♅   Experiences stimulate the personality's
      □   feelings of independence. With the
      ☍   conjunction, individuation is emphasized, quite possibly nervously; with the square, independence tends to be achieved through separation, upset, overturn; with the opposition, independence may be emphasized by the separation by someone else *from* the native.

Within a very settled birth horoscope (with a trine between Mercury and Saturn, for example), the periods of the Moon's progressed relationship with Uranus may bring the experience of personal reform, idiosyncracies set aside, fresh and efficient expression of individuality. —Definitely, these aspects indicate times of intense self-awareness.

P. ☽ ⚹ ♅   These periods will be most fortunate. The
   △   individuality flows easily and well in experience, collecting favor, endorsement, and friendship.

Moon-Neptune

P. ☽ ☌ ♆   These progressed aspects with Neptune
   □   heighten the sense perceptions, the dream
   ☍   activity, the meeting with unusual people.
Depending upon the birth condition of Neptune, high sensitivity may be expected at conjunction; self-deception or deception by others at the square and opposition.

The personality is keenly sensitive to its own mysterious interpretations of experience.

P. ☽ ⚹ ♆   The personality will benefit through its
   △   sensitivity. Meetings with unusual people may prove curiously beneficial; fortuitous coincidences.

Moon-Pluto

P. ☽ ☌ ♇   Experiences occur to highlight the
   □   individual's position within society.
   ☍   Personal perspectives are defined, challenged, or gain adjustment in relation to social organization, professional institutions, political alinement, the Self's world-concept.

P. ☽ ⚹ △ ♇ There is a passing awareness that the Self is in good position with regard to social, professional, or national dimensions in the life.

Note: If the condition of Pluto in the birth horoscope contributes to difficulty (squared by Mercury, for example), *any* progressed aspect by the Moon to Pluto (including the sextile and trine) seems to heighten awareness of this difficulty through experience.

Progressed Planetary Aspects

The planets *progress* much more slowly than the Sun and Moon. Although Mercury and Venus *move* more quickly than the Sun, their progressions can be slower because of retrograde periods. When the planets progress into periods of retrogradation, their progressed significance becomes very focused in meaning and long in duration within a particular zone or aspect to a radical planet. Then, when the progressed planet resumes direct motion during a year of development, the turning point is very dramatic in terms of past years spent in a particular zone or within a particular aspect. Similarly, when a planet becomes retrograde, the introduction of a counterpoint emphasis can be expected for a long time to come in relation to the planet's zone and aspect.

The planets apply to and separate from progressed aspects slowly. We can allow an orb of three degrees for application and separation. This six-degree arc of overall significance will always be longer than six years for Mars and Jupiter, whose motions are so slow. For Mercury and Venus, the arc may be fulfilled much sooner than six years, when retrogradation does not occur within the time span.

Most importantly, what may be suggested as potential within interplanetary progressed aspects will appear to "wait" for fulfillment *according to the Moon's accumulation of experience through its more swiftly forming progressed aspects.* To a very great extent, the progressed interplanetary aspects refer to an individual's *inclination to respond when experiences challenge the individual's developmental potential.*

☿ Mercury ☿

Mercury-Sun

When the radical Mercury progresses to a conjunction with the Sun, its condition describing the mental, perceptual, and nervous dimensions is brought directly to the condition of the Sun in the birth horoscope. Often, the conjunction occurs at too young an age to be seen conspicuously, except possibly through a change of home or extensive traveling through the parents (if Mercury refers by position, aspects, or rulership to House III, IV, IX, or X). In a young adult, this progressed conjunction brings the individual's mental faculties to an illumined and direct application through the condition of the Sun, the focus of character and life-energy. —If the Sun is in difficult aspect in the birth chart, the conjunction formed by the progressed Mercury may bring the difficulty strongly into awareness.

Mercury-Moon

The Mercury-Moon relationship is very similar to the Mercury-Sun conjunction: the mental, perceptual, and nervous dimensions of the personality are brought directly to bear upon the personality's form, needs, and cultivation of experience, especially through conjunction and opposition. The square will increase the tension factors in the fulfillment of the Moon's condition; the sextile and trine will ease this fulfillment.

Mercury-Venus

Mercury's progression to a conjunction with Venus increases the idealization dimensions within the personality. The individual will seek a mental harmony: if the birth Venus is in difficult aspect at birth, the progressed Mercury will introduce worrying, shifting of position, over-analysis in order to establish a social, romantic or aesthetic ideal. Financial concerns as well will be subject to the mind's strong attention.

Mercury-Mars

P. ☿ ♂ ☐ ♂ These progressed aspects with Mars are very ♊ important. The native's mind and nervous system, his capacity for change and reorganization are brought into strong focus, developmental tension, or keen awareness with the system's applied energy potential. Decisions are extremely important. The spirit of enterprise is awakened; there is a tendency to overwork, anxiety, hasty judgment, strain.

Eisenhower's progressed Mercury conjoined his

radical Mars in Capricorn in X (ruler of the Ascendant) at age sixty-six in 1955 through 1956: he suffered a heart attack as president (24 September 1955, progressed Moon approaching the Ascendant) and announced his availability for a second term (29 February 1956, progressed Moon reaching the Ascendant)!

P. ☿ ⚹ ♂ The native's mental faculties, flexibility,
     △   and judgment work very well through applied energy, seen through the condition of Mars in the birth horoscope.

Mercury-Jupiter

P. ☿ ☌ ♃ The intelligence is brought to the
     □
     ☍   enthusiasms of the personality; there is a preparedness for opportunity. With the conjunction, good judgment can be expected; with the square, perhaps poor judgment because of deceit, hypocrisy, or complicated legalisms; with the opposition, judgment may have difficulty stabilizing itself. —There is a flexible dimension to these aspects: with the conjunction, the native may see solutions to problems through creative ideas of change, constructive alteration of strategies; with the square, change of course might be demanded by circumstances, even by a change of locale; with the opposition, change is seen as an open-ended alternative.

At Mercury square Jupiter, Jacquline Bouvier journeyed to France for a year of study.

P. ☿ ⚹△ ♃ Expansive mental capacities invite varied

experiences for the learning process. Good judgment is natural, and successful expression is promised through writing, publishing, communicating, and travel.

Mercury-Saturn

P. ☿ ☌ ♄   Any aspect between progressed Mercury
□   and Saturn brings to the pursuit of
☍   ambition Mercury's birth-horoscope
synthesis with respect to mind and nervous system.

In the conjunction, the mind becomes sober, solemn. Should Mercury's condition at birth be problematic the progressed conjunction may correspond to depression, melancholy. —Responsibilities will be placed upon the native. A positive, uplifting progressed aspect with Jupiter elsewhere in the horoscope at the same time will help to give buoyancy to mood.

In the square, affairs of study, learning, decision, and travel may experience delay. —But the delays may be a tension for *improved* plans. Pessimism is sure to be felt, and it can be most positively interpreted as creative caution.

In the opposition, delays or frustrations may originate from others rather than from within the native.

These three progressed aspects are powerful. In a modern interpretation, they may be seen as *calls to wisdom.* Careful, painstaking judgments can solidly build ambition's pedestal.

Henry Ford founded the Detroit Motor Company with progressed Mercury conjunct Saturn. Jacqueline Kennedy gave birth to a dead baby girl; her father died;

Caroline was born; the family moved to Georgetown in the Mercury square Saturn period.

P. ☿ ✶ ♄   These aspects bring steady, thoughtful,
△   prudent, wise influences upon the intelligence and judgment. Responsibilities and detail management are welcomed and produce good results in forwarding ambition.

Mercury-Uranus

P. ☿ ♂ ♅   Intelligence and flexibility are brought to
□
☍   the service of individuality, the intensification of the Self. Unless both planets are well configurated within the birth horoscope, the aspects will be accompanied by noticeable nervousness, especially in the square.

Matters of writing, creativity, travel, change, siblings—are are brought to high focus within these periods.

Progressed Mercury and progressed Mars both opposed Jacqueline Kennedy's House V Uranus when she married Aristotle Onassis (20 October 1968) and when the Roswell Gilpatric letters were made public (Spring, 1970).

P. ☿ △ ♅   The native is possessed of originality, thoughtfulness, ingenuity; interest in the occult, especially Astrology.

Mercury-Neptune

P. ☿ ☌ ♆   The mind will subtly tend to absorb
    □   psychic, spiritual, visionary influences,
    ☍   through meditation, dreaming, occult
reading, possibly drugs. This is a time when circumstances
may be bewildering.

Depending upon the birth condition of these planets,
the absorption will be beneficial or detrimental to the sound-
ness of thinking, learning, perception, and resourcefulness.

Jacqueline Bouvier's Mercury progressed to a
conjunction with her radical Neptune in House X when she
was eleven to thirteen years old. Her parents' divorce was
finalized and her mother remarried. Charles Manson's
Mercury progressed to a square with his Neptune-Mars
conjunction in House V in 1966 through 1968, when he
began to assemble his drug-oriented, hedonistic, deluded
followers.

P. ☿ ⚹ ♆   Sensitivity can work beneficially through
    △   inspiration, artistic understanding and
communication.

Picasso's Mercury progressed to trine his Neptune in
1952 through 1953 at ages seventy-one to seventy-two,
precisely the time when he conceived and worked upon
two panels, entitled *War and Peace*, called the "most
ambitious work ever undertaken by the artist," for which
he made no fewer than 150 drawings and sketches to
clarify his inspiration.

Mercury-Pluto

P. ☿ ♂
☐
♂

This period is almost invariably marked by a great desire to study mystery, deep significances, research of the unknown or the not yet formulated. Through study, the individual applies his mind to help establish personal perspective, his own place in the world.

It is very important, especially in the progressed square aspect, that the *natal* Mercury is balanced and healthy. If the natal Mercury is debilitated, the study of mystery and the unknown, curiosity and projection can lose sight of personal perspective in reality; imbalance can displace clarification. —Often, affairs of death and mysterious occurrences are the stimuli for research and investigation.

Jacqueline Onassis' excellent natal Mercury progresses to square her natal Pluto in House VIII, ruling her Scorpio Ascendant, at age forty-seven to forty-eight in 1976 through 1977.

♀ Venus ♀

Venus-Sun: See Sun-Venus

Venus-Moon: See Moon Venus

Venus-Mercury: See Mercury-Venus

Venus-Mars

P. ♀ ☌ ♂   The progressed aspects of Venus with the
  □   radical Mars emphasize loving, socializing,
  ☍
and often financing activities; also the affections, sex
instincts, impulses, a desire for harmony, and parenthood.

The square will most often correspond to difficulties
within these emotional areas: the challenge to adjust
relationships.

The opposition often finds the person at a loss to
understand personal emotions and the gracious
administration of Venus energies. Desires can be opposed
to the will of the other person.

P. ♀ ✶ ♂   Social, love, creative, and financial
  △   concerns are easily and successfully realized
depending upon other progressed aspects in formation at
the same time.

Venus-Jupiter

P. ♀ ☌ ♃   The conjunction is a pervasive, subtle
  □   influence of good fortune and peaceful
  ☍   fulfillment. If Jupiter is very well
configurated financially in the birth horoscope, the period
will be one of definite reward.

The square brings a mixture of sorrow and pleasure:
values are shifted, lost, readjusted, improved. The
emotions expand and contract. There is usually a happy
ending to any difficulty encountered.

The opposition suggests the potential that emotional
concerns will have difficulty merging with expansion plans.

Separations may occur, e.g., traveling away from a problem. Legal matters may attach themselves to these concerns, as may possible financial difficulties.

These progressed aspects between Venus and Jupiter *accompany* the significances of other, stronger progressed aspects in formation at the same time.

P. ♀ ⚹ ♃   Pleasure, success, ease, gain, expansion are
   △   indicated by these aspects.

Hitler's vast territorial gains at the beginning of World War II were achieved during the progressed trine.

Venus-Saturn

P. ♀ ☌ ♄   The progressed aspects of Venus bring
   □   loving, socializing, and often financing
   ☍   activity *into control situations* through
Saturn. On the positive side: marriage may be indicated with a much older person; a disciplined security can be gained by a personality needing anchor and guidance; economy, thrift, and reform can stabilize the personality. On the negative side: emotions can be cut off, assets can be frozen, discipline can confine and wound; there may be bereavement.

Preparation for these periods is a safeguard that the positive side will be emphasized. With the square, intensification of feelings will be added; the tension will be greater. With the opposition, the personality may feel victimized as well. Health may suffer. —The aspects with Sautrn are *calls to economy*.

P. ♀ ✶ ♄   The sense of responsibility is high;
   △   stabilizing factors facilitate excellent gain.
There is beneficial influence from elders.

Venus-Uranus

P. ♀ ♂ ♅   Emotions and creativity are intensified.
   □   The unusual emerges to gain recognition
   ☍   for the individuality. The Self is intensified
through social relationships, affections, aesthetics,
spending.

With the conjunction, square, and opposition, there is
always the possibility of sudden change, sudden shifts of
emotional expression, crisis, separations, new starts,
challenge from others—all made to somehow define or free
individuality, to emphasize it uniquely or stress its
independence.

The significances of Venus and Uranus in the birth
chart come together strongly and can appear to create a
powerful force separate from the rest of the horoscope!
The meaning of this "electric" aspect can run away with
the personality.

President Nixon's progressed Venus squares Uranus in
1971 through 1973; Venus rules Libra on II (finances),
Taurus on IX (ethics); progressed Venus in VIII (other
peoples' resources); birth Venus in VI (service, colleague
relationships).

P. ♀ ✶ ♅   Gain is possible through highly individual
   △   emotional behavior, friends, study. There is

great openness to suggestion, influence, and sudden developments.

Venus-Neptune

P. ♀ ♂ ♅ These aspects suggest high emotional
   □ sensitivity; aesthetic susceptibility, need for
   ☍
idealization.

At conjunction, the influence is felt internally, psychically, religiously, aesthetically. At the square, surreal sensitivity is developed through a tension from outside, a "calling," a highly unusual friend, a lofty institution; the personality has less control for efficient assimilation of the influences.

At the opposition, the highly sensitive personality may experience a period of self-delusion emotionally and often financially.

The "settled" personality may respond only slightly to the aspects: a slight magnification of emotions, some religious thought, a need to express one's self, perhaps delusion by others.

When Nixon's Venus progressed to a square with Neptune in 1962, he wrote his book *Six Crises*, reviewing his political career after having lost the presidential election.

P. ♀ ⚹ ♅ These aspects indicate an extremely
   △ positive time of fulfillment, joy, freedom
of expression, rare experience.

Lyndon Johnson was elected to the presidency by the

largest percentage of popular votes ever in 1964 with progressed Venus (ruler of Midheaven) sextile Neptune in XI.

Venus-Pluto

P. ♀ ☌ ♇ Emotions—socialization, aesthetics,
　□　　love—are brought into developmental
　☍　　relationship with the individual's sense of personal and professional perspective. Group affiliation and institutional employment may become very important in life.

Romance, investment, projections of ambition all take on grander perspective. —If the radical Pluto contributes to difficult aspect structures, the emotions may be "taken in" by unlawful or underground lures.

P. ♀ ⚹ ♇ The personality benefits from an awareness
　△　　of expansion of Venus-dimensions.

If the radical Venus is debilitated, *any* progressed aspect with Pluto (sextile and trine included) will tend to accent emotional difficulty.

♂ Mars ♂

Mars-Sun

Mars-Sun progressed aspects are similar to Sun-Mars aspects; the birth condition of the personality's applied energy is brought to the significances of the Sun's birth Sign and House, the "heart of the matter."

The conjunction accompanies a high focus of ego strength: Nixon married.

The square accompanies extreme developmental tension, possible failing health, surgery, recklessness, impulse, etc.

The opposition suggests a period of drastic turn-over of the status quo and vigorous new beginning.

The sextile and trine suggest terrific self-application, successful drive, and personal vitality.

Mars-Moon

These progressed aspects are similar to Moon-Mars *and* Mars-Sun aspects with the addition that, in a male horoscope, a woman in the native's life may be involved in events (conjunction), developmental tension or illness (square), and separation or attack (opposition).

For all horoscopes, the conjunction, square, and opposition from the progressed Mars to the Moon mark periods of extreme drive, danger to health, possible surgery, and a demand for recognition.

The sextile and trine promise easy personality development through energy expression and public endorsement; also a high vitality.

John F. Kennedy experienced the progressed conjunction of Mars to Venus, square the Moon, between the ages of thirty-nine and forty-one: he had his second spinal operation, was awarded the Pulitzer Prize for Literature, his daughter Caroline was born, and he was reelected to the Senate (Moon ruled the Cancer

Midheaven; Mars ruled VII; Venus ruled the Ascendant).

Mars-Mercury

Mars energies conditioned by its birth position are brought to Mercury in its position: House, Sign, aspects, rulerships. The conjunction, square, and opposition heighten the nervous system, the thinking process, communication of all kinds. The square may suggest the possibility of travel accidents; the opposition may suggest strong disagreements from others within experiences.

The sextile and trine indicate ease of communication, contract fulfillments, benefits from travel, etc. (See Mercury-Mars.)

Mars-Venus: See Venus-Mars

Mars-Jupiter

P. ♂ ☌ ♃ Pride is a powerful dimension during the
　　□　　period of conjunction. Ostentation and
　　☍　　exuberant extravagance threaten to waste
rewards. Ability must be anchored by prudence to fulfill the goals indicated. Horizons are expanded by marriage.

The square will accentuate the dimensions mentioned in the preceding paragraph, with the addition of nervous thrust. The scope of the goal can exceed the capacity of the energies: litigation may threaten as society tries to curb the expansive energies.

The opposition threatens real problems from overzealous application of Self: in financial matters, travel, bargaining, inflated planning, reckless expansion. —The progressed aspects of the Moon are very important in synthesizing the progressed aspects of Mars to Jupiter. The Moon's aspects will show the response of the environment to the native's enthusiastic press of luck. A stabilizing aspect with Saturn will help provide anchor.

Einstein was awarded the Nobel Prize for Physics at the conjunction (Jupiter in Aquarius, House IX, square Pluto in the birth horoscope). Eisenhower married at the conjunction.

P. ♂ ✳ ♃   The natures of Mars and Jupiter never
    △   achieve complete compatibility. Even in sextile and trine, although liberality and generosity are suggested, there is always the danger of overdoing, i.e., of too much of a good thing.

Travel will be beneficial, but there may be the need to do too much; emotions will be expanded healthfully, but perhaps over too broad an area.

The aspects call for *technique* to guide energies to fulfill opportunities. Careful investments can pay off handsomely. With perspective, the feelings are lifted to new levels and horizons are beneficially expanded.

Jacqueline Kennedy's Mars trined her Jupiter in the period of 1966 through 1968: controversy over the Manchester book; trip to Cambodia; trip to Mexico; assassination of Robert Kennedy (5 June 1968); marriage to Aristotle Onassis (20 October 1968).

Mars-Saturn

P. ♂ ♂ ♄　　Mars energy comes into highest focus with
□　　　　ambition. The conjunction can emphasize
♂　　　　Mars *or* Saturn. The blend is very difficult
to achieve. There is the danger of high temperament and
demand within all the aspects; and the danger of depressed
melancholy and withdrawal. —The objective should be to
avoid bad judgment (especially at the square) through
proper perspective of ambition's course and energy's
potential.

These aspects mark a critical challenge to the system
out of which can be forged progress of steel, when
impulses do not overcome caution, when caution does not
overcome energy. The aspects mark a *call to strategy*.

Lyndon Johnson won the presidency by a landslide in
1964 at the applying opposition of Mars and Saturn (and
progressed Venus trine Neptune), and announced that he
would not seek renomination when the opposition was
exact in 1968. —The square aspect dominated Hitler's last
years, withdrawal, and death.

P. ♂ ✶ ♄　　The blend between Mars and Saturn at best
△　　　　is never complete; hot meets cold. The
progressed aspects of the Moon will be extremely
important to suggest the receptivity of the environment to
the aggressive drive of the system. Under good conditions,
the period can be monumental. Under threatening
conditions, authority will have to give way to wise counsel
to help the fulfillment of ambition, entirely possible at
these times.

Mars-Uranus

P. ♂ ♂ ♅   Mars stimulates the individuality to its
□   highest response: nerves, egotism, thrust,
♂   drive, innovation, sudden changes. The
spirit of invention, creativity, mechanical operations are all
invigorated by these aspects.

The conjunction seems to "invite" sudden,
unexpected events that challenge the system and bring
opportunity for great progress. In very sensitive
horoscopes, a dimension of psychic awareness,
inspirational intuition may lead to sudden innovation and
action. This is a period of extremely high tension.

The square is vigorously demanding: the feelings will
be highly stressed. Fire, electricity, speed, travel, risks
should be avoided with great care. —Enforced calm is
necessary.

The opposition will usually accompany a complete
reorganization of personal affairs (through the House of
Uranus especially). The individual will feel attacked by his
society, his friends, his partner. —Sex can play a vital role
in all these Mars-Uranus aspects.

At the conjunction, Nixon was reelected vice
president and toured Latin America (stoned and vilified).
At the square, Lyndon Johnson died of a heart attack
(January 22, 1973, midnight); Henry Ford founded the
Ford Motor Company. At the opposition, Jacqueline
Onassis was hounded by newsmen, photographers, and
books about her private life and the first years of her
marriage to Onassis; arguments, separations, and tension
were rumored in the public media (1970 through 1972).

P. ♂ ⚹ ♅   A favorable period for practical effort and
△   the use of creative methods,. Unusual
friends will benefit the native. Personal magnetism is high.

The trine is exceptionally powerful, easily lifting the potentials of inspiration to the level of applied genius.

Mars-Neptune

P. ♂ ☌ ♆   The higher faculties of existence are
□   emphasized. At conjunction, new
☍   inspiration and idealization are possible.

At square, inspiration is sought; self-delusion is possible (drugs, alcohol); energies can take strange directions to fulfill turbulent desires; violence is possible through a distorted value system.

At the opposition, too much is expected from existence, leading to frustration, isolation, inexplicable feelings.

In a down-to-earth horoscope with few sensitivity dimensions accentuated, the progressed aspects may bring an unconscious magnetism to the personality, higher energies for attracting self-fulfillment. Nixon began his political career in the House of Representatives during the opposition at age thirty-three, in 1946.

P. ♂ ⚹ ♆   These aspects indicate periods of ease in
△   enjoying life, new life, unusual life;
understanding higher values of friendship and the spirit. A personal magnetism prevails.

Truman was reelected president, defeating heavy

odds, when sixty-three to sixty-five, during the period of the trine, 1947 through 1949.

Mars-Pluto

P. ♂ ♂ ♇ Applied energies in development invigorate
    □   perspective, activity within social and
    ♂   professional structures, self-assertiveness.
Especially at conjunction, the personality "feels" its position most clearly, perhaps too clearly—with pleasure or upset.

At the square, passionate desires may be excited; there is an acquisitive drive for power and expansion; impulsive actions can disrupt the status quo.

At the opposition, argumentative outbursts arouse antagonisms, separation, abandonment.

Affairs of death may be involved in all three of these periods; also dimensions of personal reformation.

Lindbergh made his record-breaking flight across the Atlantic when progressed Mars squared his radical Pluto.

P. ♂ ⚹ ♇ A subtle correspondence may be expected:
    △   social, professional, and personal standards,
perspective, and scope of application are easily clarified by experience.

Jupiter ♃ Saturn ♄ Uranus ♅ Neptune ♆ Pluto ♇

Jupiter, Saturn, and the outer planets progress only a few degrees by Secondary Progressions during a lifetime. Any aspect formed in progression can surely be interpreted in terms of application to the aspect seen through the aspect's orb at birth.

Midheaven and Ascendant

Progressions of the Midheaven bring very important focus of the whole life's development into a particular birth planet position and configuration. For the young, progression of the Midheaven will correspond to positions within House X, emphasizing alterations in life through the parents or the earliest professional positions (especially with radical Saturn in X). For the adult, the Midheaven usually progresses out of X into XI and further, bringing an emphasis of profession and personal honor into particular birth planet positions and configurations originating in House XI: goals, wishes, love-received, friendships; the creativity of the partner; children's affairs; financial objectives.

Progression of the Ascendant most often heightens self-awareness in terms of the birth planet and aspect configurations involved. Powerful awareness of potentials, seen through the planets, is established at conjunction; strong developmental change at the square; awareness at the opposition; ease and support of expression at the trine and sextile. —This author began his writing career in Astrology when the progressed Ascendant conjoined Pluto, opposed Mercury in Capricorn in VIII, and squared Mars simultaneously.

Apparently, the progression of the Ascendant into a Sign different from the Ascendant's Sign at birth is significant. The Self's projection and receptivity to experience are changed to include the significance of the Sign of the progressed Ascendant.

A Sign is divided into thirds: ten degrees each. These thirds are called *decanates*. Each decanate (group of ten degrees) within a Sign has a different subtle characteristic within the overall characteristic of the whole Sign ... very easily learned.

For example: Aries-Leo-Sagittarius are the three Signs of the Fire Family. We think of them always in this order: Cardinal (Aries), Fixed (Leo), and Mutable (Sagittarius). The decanates of any Sign always follow this same order as well. For Aries

- the first decanate, first ten degrees, is ruled by Mars;
- the second decanate, second ten degrees (Aries 10 to Aries 19), refers subtly to the Leo characteristics of the Element Family. The second decanate will be sub-ruled by the Sun, ruler of Leo;
- the third decanate, last ten degrees (Aries 20 to Aries 29), refers subtly to the Sagittarius characteristics of the Element Family. The third decanate will be sub-ruled by Jupiter, ruler of Sagittarius.

Similarly, the first decanate of Leo is ruled by the Sun; the second decanate is sub-ruled by Jupiter, ruler of Sagittarius; the third decanate is sub-ruled by Mars, ruler of Aries.

The reference of the decanate progresses successively

through the Element Family, in order: Cardinal-Fixed-Mutable; Fixed-Mutable-Cardinal; Mutable-Cardinal-Fixed.

The significance of the decanate of the progressed Ascendant should be interpreted in terms of the sub-ruling planet, the *natural* House location of the Sign ruled by this planet, and the condition of this sub-ruling planet in the actual birth horoscope.

For example: Nixon's progressed chart for thirty-seven years, the time of his election as Senator (page 66) shows a progressed Ascendant at 20 Libra 09, the third decanate of Libra, sub-ruled by *Mercury* (Gemini Decanate: Libra-Aquarius-*Gemini*). Therefore, while the progressed Ascendant is in the last ten degrees of Libra, the significance of Libra and of Mercury and its Signs Gemini and Virgo—and their natural references to Houses III and VI—will be suggested in the background of all developmental experience. For Nixon, this is very clear, involving through his progressed Ascendant the Sign Gemini on his radical Midheaven and Virgo on his radical Ascendant, House III and VI affairs as well, and the sub-ruler Mercury ... in addition to Venus, ruler of Libra ... and soon in the future the square between this progressed Ascendant in detailed analysis and the radical Neptune.

The progressed decanate is a very subtle and often very reliable measurement. It will enter our subsequent studies when particularly relevant.

Additional Considerations

The orb of application of progressed aspects to birth planets is shorter than the orbs for the aspects made by the

Sun, Moon, and planets in the birth horoscope. One should allow an application of only one degree—at most two degrees—a time of partile (exactness) of one degree, and a separation of one degree for all progressed aspects except those made by the Moon. This means that, for the Sun, about three years will be involved in the significance of the aspect: approximately one year in building, one year in high focus, and one year in waning. Application and separation for the planets through the three-degree arc will usually be significantly longer.

For the Moon, application and separation orbs may be considerably extended since one degree always approximates one *month* of progressed time.

Several progressed aspects will usually be in different phases of fulfillment at the same time. The "trigger" for the whole manifestation is usually dependent upon the progressed Moon: potentials seem to "wait" for the Moon to make strong aspects before manifesting themselves. —The time period of application, focus, and separation, keyed by the Moon, is easily and creatively clarified through dialogue with the individual.

When the Sun comes to the cusp of a new house, *the cusp position itself* may be symbolically regarded as a point of very important focus. The Sun will appear to apply to the cusp and enter the new fields of life development promised by the particular House. An orb of one degree or two degrees application to the cusp within an accurately timed birth horoscope will be conspicuously valid in interpretation.

Similarly, for the Sun and the planets, when they

enter a new Sign by progression, their progressed interpretations take on the significances of the new Sign also. —For the Moon, the significance of the zone of experience, the House, is much more important than the Sign.

In the same way that the Sun is especially significant when crossing the House cusp line, so progressed planets *in aspect with the Ascendant and Midheaven* should be carefully interpreted. An aspect to the radical Midheaven will involve the profession, the reputation, perhaps one of the parents, the self-esteem, etc.; to the radical Ascendant, the personality projection, health, whole orientation, style of expression.

Health. It is very important to understand that development in life *affects the entire organism.* Experience and the passage of time have an effect upon the health of the personality's body and nervous system. During a particularly stressful period, the organism is challenged to do more, to be more, to fulfill potentials perhaps by altering course. Change disrupts order; the health may be affected whether or not House VI references are involved within the birth horoscope. For example, at a time of ambitious expansion (progressed Moon square Saturn), a nervous rash, teeth problems, or stomach upset may occur. One may literally and figuratively have "weak knees" (Saturn rules the knees)! —The Sun and Leo will place attention upon the heart, spine, and circulation; Mercury and Uranus, Gemini and Aquarius, will involve the nervous system, especially in aspect with Mars; Venus and Libra, the kidneys, the hair, the throat (Taurus); Mars and Aries, fever, headaches, temper, accident; Jupiter and Virgo, the liver, the diet, intestines; Saturn, the skin, teeth, bones, melancholy, chill, aging; Neptune and Pluto, Pisces and Scorpio, the blood, "cold feet", sexual organs; the Moon and Cancer, the stomach, public image, self-esteem. (These health significances will be studied thoroughly in Volume IX of this series, *Special Horoscope Dimensions: Success, Sex, Illness.*)

Minor aspects. Before the discovery of the trans-Saturnian planets, the quest to relate Astrological correspondences to experience necessitated the formalization of *minor* aspects in addition to the major conjunction, sextile, square, trine, and opposition. Indeed, any and every relationship between the planets within the horoscope must surely be significant within the order of the system. Aspects have been formulated that, through their orbs, do cover the entire circle.

Again, we meet indeterminateness: man simply cannot assimilate the whole order completely; an infinitesimally detailed correspondence eludes man's relativity systems. Yet, minor aspects do contribute to the whole picture at times and should be noted by the student for occasional application in the birth chart and in progressed aspects. Hereafter in the series, minor aspects will be noted in analysis when they are significant:

⋎ semi-sextile, 30 degrees (one Sign), growth.

∠ semi-square, 45 degrees (one Sign plus 15 degrees), friction.

⊡ sesqui-quadrate, 135 degrees (trine plus 15 degrees), minor upset.

⚻ quincunx, 150 degrees (five Signs; one less than opposition), development.

Additionally, progressed parallels of declination should be noted when constructing the horoscope for the Secondary Progression date. Often, the progressed parallel will be helpful corroboration of deductions in synthesis, especially that between Venus and Mars, suggesting an emphasis upon sex within the period.

The aspects between progressed planets and other progressed planets are particularly important, especially between the progressed Sun or Ascendant ruler and the progressed Mars. These should always be noted and interpreted accordingly.

Converse progressions. There are theorists who have applied Secondary Progressions *backwards* in time to measure development in the future! These are called converse Secondary Progressions: days *before* birth are counted *backwards* from the date of birth to arrive at the converse progression date. For Nixon's thirty-seventh year, the converse progression would be to 3 December 1912 (thirty-seven days before birth): the converse Venus was applying to conjunction with the radical Sun; the converse Moon was applying to conjunction with the Part of Fortune, trine the Midheaven and radical Moon; the converse Mars was square the radical Venus; the previous New Moon lunation, the converse New Moon—new light in the life—had occurred five years earlier (converse date, December 8) exactly conjunct Nixon's fourth cusp at 16 Sagittarius (!), when Nixon began his political career in the House of Representatives.

Converse progressions seem to have relevance. The time and space continuum of the birth horoscope again defies actual future time calculation; it can be delineated by so many different systems of man's invention *without* reference to actual time. Man's approximations through radix direction, rapport measurement, factor-7 analysis, Secondary Progressions, and converse progressions appear to define the whole more clearly with every system, with every measurement.

It is with *transits* that *actual* time is integrated within the approximations developed out the birth horoscope through the various systems. Transits measure the actual time and space positions of the planets, the influence of the actual environment. The next volume in this series, number VII, *Integrated Transits,* studies the placement of actual time measurement within the background potentials established through directions, progressions, and rapport deductions.

Terminal Theory. With the very slow progression of Jupiter, Saturn, Uranus, Neptune, and Pluto, we may note a method of measuring more extensively the time element of their significances, of articulating more meaningfully the arc of progression: if the progressed Moon squares the radical Saturn and corresponding strong development occurs in life experience (and almost invariably it will!), the significance is not simply confined to the orb of approach, partile, and separation; the developments will certainly last longer or require a longer period to be worked out and assimilated by the system. We can note Saturn's *progressed position* perhaps two or three degrees further on and extend the period of the progressed Moon's application, partile, and separation to and from the progressed Saturn as well. This will extend the period significantly. If the occurrence at the radical aspect is exceptionally strong, the effects of the experiences can be projected forward until the Moon separates completely from aspect with the progressed Saturn. —The radical position and the progressed position of Saturn, in this case, are called *terminals;* the terminals are poles that define the entire experience-arc in terms of time, the breadth of the expanded present.

If the progressed Saturn has *retrograded* during the life so that its progressed position is behind (in lesser longitude than) the radical position, the Moon will aspect the *progressed* Saturn before it aspects the *radical* Saturn. The arc of time and development will begin at the *progressed* Saturn (retrograde) terminal and gain in strength to aspect with the radical terminal.

Terminal theory of measurement applies best to aspects made by the Moon to Jupiter and the planets beyond. In many circumstances, the Sun's progression can be expanded through terminal theory in aspect to these same planets, but the experience manifested at the first terminal must be strong enough to justify extension of the arc to the second terminal.

For exact measurements, each progressed planet's progressed daily motion (motion for the progressed year) may be subdivided by dividing the daily motion by twelve to determine the position each month. As explained on page 70, this is essential for the Moon and it is a very easy matter. For the Sun and other planets, subdivision is rarely needed.

Some researchers place much emphasis upon the Houses of the *progressed* horoscope. —At best, this appears to be of very minor significance except in rare cases. With experience, the progressed Houses can be approximated easily from the progressed planets in relation to the progressed Ascendant and the progressed Midheaven *as noted upon the radix.*

Speed Calculation. Construction of the progressed horoscope can be done much more quickly than construction of the radix, *after* the birth horoscope has been completed. *The daily motions of the planets will more often than not be approximately the same on the progressed date as on the birth date.* The motion increment from noon to the GMT birth time has already been computed and noted on the work sheet for each planet in the birth horoscope. It is a very simple matter to check the daily motion of a planet on the progressed date just by looking at the notation in the Ephemeris and, if it is quite close to the motion on the birth date, quickly add the same increment to the noon position of the progressed planet! However, special care must be given to Mercury and Venus, whose motions can vary considerably, and to any change to retrograde or direct motion. —The motion and increment of the progressed Moon must be computed exactly in every case.

With practice, the erection of the progressed horoscope and placement of the progressed planets around the radix takes only three to five minutes. —For the progressed Midheaven, simply add the number of progressed years in degrees to the radical Midheaven, mark it on the radix; then, in the *Tables of Houses* look *under the birth latitude* for the progressed Midheaven (the same number of lines as years after the birth line in the *Tables*) and note the progressed Ascendant listed for that progressed Midheaven. *Computing the sidereal time corrections for the progressed horoscope is not necessary!*

Radix directions can be computed on sight or, using the Sepharial refinements, with minimum pencil work. The rapport measurements can be made at a glance. The factor-7 projections can be made from the Table of Aspects on the horoscope sheet, if the student employs the same ordering of aspects as used in this series: the grid at the lower left of complete horoscopes, noting the aspects *and the orb* of the aspects. The orb is the key: multiplied by seven, development begins to suggest itself through consummation at partile.

After the birth horoscope is drawn and radix interrelationships are noted, the astrologer immediately has a feel of the whole. Approximations of progressions are made, and the feel begins to order itself in time measurement. Then, the progressed positions are noted very easily and placed around the radix. The time and development portrait begins to grow.

On the horoscope sheet, the astrologer should note the major progressed aspects in formation at the progressed time, beginning with the Sun, the ruler of the Sun-Sign, the ruler of the Ascendant, and then the other planets; retrograde or direct motion shifts, parallels; Midheaven; Ascendant decanate. Then, the progressed Moon aspects should be noted by month throughout the progressed year. —The whole begins to emerge.

Example 1: Private Case
Progression for 50th year

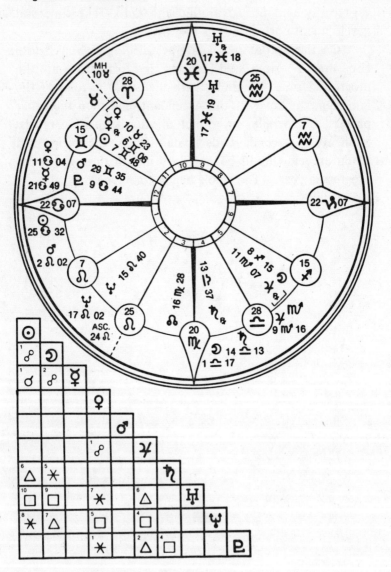

6

Progressed Aspects in Analysis

The horoscope on the facing page shows an exact Full Moon birth, Sun in Gemini (27-minute orb). From Volume III of this series, the Sun-Moon blend description reads:

> Information, travel, adventure, imagination... all gain focus in this polarity. Reactions at vastly separate levels await a bond with support-and-development aspects within the horoscope. The nervous, intellectual thrust has trouble realizing the lofty, far-reaching philosophies. Gossip or idle chit-chat can fill in the gap. Talking about goals can substitute for realization of them. A hard person to pin down. The mind works overtime and can run away into several directions at once unless anchored into concentration. Then, tremendous achievement is possible: from the academic to the spiritual.

The man came to this astrologer two months after his fiftieth birthday. He is the director of several companies within a large conglomerate. It is immediately obvious that he enjoys the "support-and-development" of Uranus square the Sun-Moon axis: he has traveled to practically every country of central and northern Europe, South America, the United States, and Russia. He speaks four languages superbly and has working knowledge of three others. —The tremendous Gemini-Sagittarius polarity is constantly fulfilling itself with reference to Uranus powerfully placed in the international House IX. His nervous system is also highly keyed through the T Cross in Mutable Signs (Volume IV), discharging into House III, communications, travel, and mental faculties. His reactions to life development are well anchored, supported, and eased through the sextile by the Moon with Saturn, the trine by the Sun and Mercury with Saturn. He is a wise man.

The executive's fantasy is occupied with money acquisition, international expansion through his several businesses (Neptune in II, ruling duality Midheaven, sextiled by the Sun, trined by the Moon, squared by Jupiter in the speculation House V that is ruled by Venus placed in Taurus, opposing Jupiter, square Neptune).

The Cancer Ascendant "softens" the nervous drive and signals the importance of the home, introducing reference to Saturn in House IV. Saturn's retrogradation will suggest change in (and throughout) the life at critical times, led by ambition; i.e., when ambition will be emphasized, the home will surely change significantly at the same time. This is especially so here since Mercury, ruler of Virgo on IV, is also retrograde and is in its own Sign (Gemini) conjunct the Sun. —Retrogradation will always indicate potential change (to direct motion) when the life is considered in a time scheme of development. The progressed positions in the outer circle are for his fiftieth birthday year. The interpretation of the progressed positions is extremely easy in the light of the capsule analysis above.

• Progressed *Mercury* is conjunct *Cancer* Ascendant; Mercury rules the Sun Sign and Virgo on *IV*. The progressed *Moon* is in *IV*. The Sun has progressed into *Cancer* and is with Mars in I.

Blending Mercury's significance of "moving," adjustment, and flexibility with the accentuation of the home through Cancer and the references to House IV, the astrologer was immediately able to ask if a new home was being planned. Had the decision for a new home been made eleven months earlier (when the Moon crossed the fourth cusp)? —This was precisely the case.

A bit further: nine months after the decision to buy a new house was made, the progressed Moon made a square to the radical Mars in XII: we would expect a problem period. Radical Mars in XII suggests disputes with organizations. The progression of the man's Moon square to this Mars suggested a tension with an organization in the development of buying a house. —This had been the case exactly: the man's applied energy to buy the house had been momentarily thwarted, made difficult by a bank. His impulses had been blocked and were resolved when he figured out a way around the difficulties.

The date planned for the move was exactly five

months after the fiftieth birthday when the progressed Moon would trine the radical Mercury-Sun and sextile its own radical position.

• *At the same time,* focus upon the profession is indicated by the Midheaven's progression to conjunction with Venus (Venus is exalted in Pisces placed upon the Midheaven); Neptune's relevance to the Sun-Moon axis and square with Venus; the Moon's applying to progressed conjunction with Saturn within the next twelve months.

The native corroborated his concerns within his business, his preparations for expansion and a move to gain more control of his companies. —The Moon would apply to a progressed square with Pluto in XII. Experiences were to occur to highlight the native's position within society, defining his personal perspectives. He feared another executive's work would limit him (XII). This situation would come to a focus eight months after the fiftieth birthday, when the progressed Moon-Pluto aspect would be exact.

• Additionally, a third dimension was deduced within this important period through the accentuation of Venus by the progressed Midheaven, Venus' approach to a progressed square with Saturn, and its progressed position within Cancer, having crossed over Pluto within the last three years, and, through Venus, the introduced focus upon House V (Libra and Scorpio). Venus in the birth chart makes a double-approaching opposition with retrograde Jupiter in V. The Moon is in V. —The native was very concerned about his children, both of whom are very bright but unusually retiring, aloof, uncommunicating (a frustration to this articulate Gemini). The native has a nervous preoccupation to organize his children's lives, to lift them to his own inordinate expressivity and constant activity. —This dimension had prompted the change of home, to bring the children into a new neighborhood (Mercury).

The analysis and counsel went much further than this capsule, of course, but this abbreviated description of the clear progressed aspects serves well for a study of Mercury, Venus, the Ascendant and Midheaven, and Houses IV and V.

Additionally, the Ephemeris indicated that the radical retrograde Saturn had resumed direct motion when the native turned twenty-one and surely left home and felt his ambition freed into tremendous international activity. He had left home at twenty, joined the armed forces in World War II, and immediately won enormous achievement, honor, and recognition in foreign service.

During the war, the native was severely injured in a sudden explosion. His arm was amputated (Gemini; Mars, Uranus): the progressed Sun was conjunct Mars; progressed Mars squared Saturn; progressed Moon squared the Sun and Mercury; the progressed Sun paralleled progressed Mars; progressed Moon paralleled progressed Uranus.

Further into the future after the fiftieth birthday, the time of consultation, one notes that the progressed Midheaven will square the radical Neptune in II in five

Example 2: Private Case
Progression for 54th year

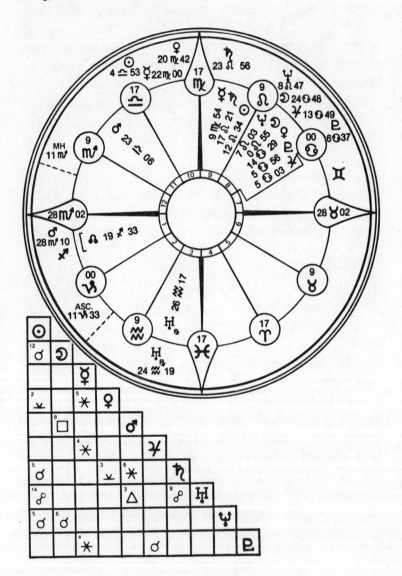

years, the Sun will enter Leo: the native will be ascending to a tremendous leadership position but not without financial delusion or camouflage within the profession. (His past revealed frequent legal battles—Venus opposed Jupiter retrograde—over withheld funds and speculation rewards.) The factor-7 measurement to partile of the Sun-Neptune sextile measures a little under eight degrees, fifty-six years. Then, the Moon will be progressing to an opposition with Mars, two years later crossing the seventh cusp. —Analysis would begin again at a new present in the future, based upon projections clarified in experience and plan at fifty.

The birth horoscope on page 158 has an unusual distribution: there are no planets in Angles and only one square within orb (Moon-Mars). The native has strong ambition, is inherently a leader (Saturn, Sun, Moon in Leo), but lacks initiative. He is constrained by disciplines (Sun conjunct Saturn, Moon in VIII conjunct Neptune; House VIII concentration). His passive nature, however will demand respect (Leo, Fixed-Sign emphasis, Scorpio Ascendant; Jupiter and Pluto, rulers of the Signs within the Ascendant, in conjunction in VIII). This is a man best employed in positions of trust and unwavering stolidity within large organizations.

Mercury is the most elevated planet, is dignified in its own Sign, Virgo, and is in sextile with the two Ascendant rulers and Venus, ruler of Libra holding Mars. The native's mind will work very well with detail professionally, without show and very perceptively. —The man was director of an accounting firm (Saturn ruling II; Mercury ruling X; House VIII emphasis on other people's resources; Uranus in its own Sign in Mercury's natural House III, trine with Mars in wide opposition with the Sun).

The native's silent strengths are open to victimization since self-assertiveness is weak. This is corroborated by the high emphasis of the southern hemisphere, the experience hemisphere above the horizon.

The singular square in the horoscope puts powerful focus upon Mars. The factor-7 analysis of Moon-Mars suggests an emphasis at age fifty-four years and eleven months. —The client sought astrological help during a crisis, six months after his fifty-fourth birthday: he was the focal center of an enormous fraud exposé within his firm. From the point of view of the public, House XI holding Mars is the *speculation fifth* of VII.

The progressed horoscope is drawn for the fifty-fourth year. Mars has come precisely to conjunction with the Ascendant, square Uranus (singleton, alone below the horizon in III, the ninth of VII, public ethics); the Sun, Mercury, and Venus have progressed into the "open," into an Angle at the Midheaven. The progressed Midheaven squares the Sun from XII (professional tension; other people's resources, institutional limitations; hidden enemies; threat of imprisonment).

The progressed Moon has returned precisely to its birth position at the time of the crisis, having squared the radical Mars seven months earlier when the troubles undoubtedly began. —The progressed Sun, in a position of high potential for honor, achievement, and recognition squares the radical Pluto and Jupiter, rulers of the

Ascendant! The conversed Midheaven squares the radical Mars!

This is a crisis chart in every detail, and the natural weaknesses of the native were not able to fight the circumstance. The innate pride and honesty prevailed, victimization was felt, and enormous disruption, career ruin, and deepest emotional hurt followed.

Significant transits accompanied this complex of progressed indications. —It was definitely a time for dramatic change of course in life development.

This situation could have been seen a few years earlier! As the progressed aspects began to form, the worst could have been anticipated; perhaps the native could have taken special precautions, exerted special controls within his firm. —Out of the crisis, it was important to salvage dignity for the Leo and look forward to a new business in a new location, at the time when the progressed Moon would conjoin the Sun and Saturn in House IX (within the following eighteen months), surely far away from the scene of the problem. The progressed Sun was applying to a sextile with Neptune, ruler of IV, new beginnings; progressed Jupiter was applying to a conjunction with Venus, ruler of XI, new goals, and VI, new work-service situations. Mercury paralleled Venus. The second decanate of the progressed Ascendant referred to Taurus-*Venus*.

On page 162 is the birth chart of Harry Truman, born 8 May 1884, at 3:43 PM at 94 West, 37 North. The

Example 3: Harry S. Truman
May 8, 1884; 3:43 PM; 94 W - 37 N
Progression for 61st year; date: July 8, 1884

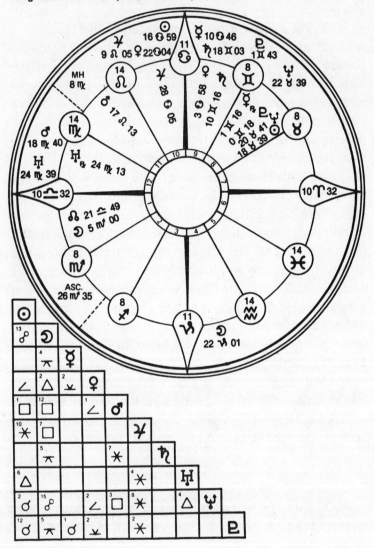

progressed chart indicated in the outer circle is drawn for his sixty-first birthday year, beginning in May 1945 (S.P. date, 8 July 1884).

Truman had just experienced a tremendous new beginning: the Moon had crossed his fourth cusp eleven months earlier in summer of 1944 when he was surprisingly nominated vice president to Franklin D. Roosevelt.

Truman's birth Sun-Neptune conjunction in VIII, trine with Uranus in XII; the natal Moon, ruling the Midheaven from the Ascendant, trine Venus, ruler of VIII; Mercury, ruler of XII, also in VIII in conjunction with Pluto, ruler of the Moon's Sign—all these references suggested through the radix that Truman would benefit powerfully during his life through the resources of others, through death situations and inheritance. Jupiter in X sextile Sun-Neptune and Uranus completed the picture. All the bodies were above the horizon, except for the Moon: Truman's openness, extraversion, full participation within experience during development. The square between Mars and Sun-Neptune in a Fixed Sign showed his driving stubbornness. The Moon in Scorpio below the horizon, within the Ascendant, suggested the very deep, sensitive, discerning personality that was rarely shown to the public and has been revealed only recently in post-mortem biography.

Upon Roosevelt's death, Truman was immediately sworn in as president: 12 April 1945, one month after his sixty-first birthday (the progressed chart), only months after becoming vice president. The progressed Moon was trine the Neptune-Sun in VIII and trine Uranus in XII. The progressed Sun, Venus, and Jupiter were within X (the Sun had crossed the Midheaven six years before when Truman first came to national prominence and then was reelected Senator); the Sun was sextile its own position; progressed Jupiter sextiled Saturn; the progressed Midheaven squared Saturn; the progressed Ascendant trined Jupiter in X; Mercury was conjunct the Midheaven, progressed from the House VIII conjunction with Pluto.

The progressed Ascendant was in the third decanate of *Scorpio,* calling attention to Pluto and the decanate ruler, the Moon.

An extremely powerful time astrologically, with every measurement suggesting tremendous new beginning, high honor and benefit publicly gained through unusual matters, perhaps matters of death and inheritance.

Transits corroborated this momentous occasion precisely.

Immediately after installment as president, Truman faced a tremendous challenge: the atomic bomb and its use. One reads today of Truman's difficult struggle with the ethical concerns of the bomb; before and after use of it on Hiroshima, 6 August 1945, the progressed Moon opposed Jupiter (professional ethics under conscious tension) from IV (homeland, patriotism for a president); Jupiter (humanity concerns) was in the Moon's natal Sign in the birth chart.

Astrology gives rulership of the atomic bomb to Pluto. At the time of Truman's deployment of the bomb, progressed Pluto was in exact conjunction with Mercury in

VIII. The natal conjunction had closed to powerful exactness at that time!

By radix projection (adding sixty one degrees or a little less) and rapport measurement: the Moon opposed Venus, ruler of VIII; Neptune sextiled the Sun in VIII; Pluto sextiled Mercury in VIII and squared the Moon; the Ascendant opposed Saturn. —By factor-7 measurement, Mercury applied to the conjunction with Saturn in nine degrees, at age sixty-one.

The horoscope on page 166 is that of a thirty-two-year-old married woman. The Sun in Pisces, Moon in Cancer (especially with the Sun-Neptune opposition) suggests fantasy, intuition, lush emotionalism; the possibility of a martyr-complex springing from a deep reservoir of ego-awareness. These feelings are expanded by the Moon's square with Jupiter and the Sun's trine with Pluto. Houses II, VIII, and VII are accentuated. The activity in House IV suggests extreme nervous tension about individuality in the home. The fantasy opposition that holds all planets within it combined with the heavy accentuation of the northern hemisphere (Neptune and Pluto retrograde above the horizon) suggests that the native has great difficulty in being happy with reality, the reality of her home, marriage, and husband.

Saturn in in square with the Moon: the native revealed that she "hated" her father. Saturn in Aries suggests defensiveness about personal ambitions. The marriage was a flight from the father's home. The tension had been transferred to her husband (Saturn square Pluto in VII); in her thirty-second year, after years of stoic

Example 4: Private Case
Progression for 32nd year

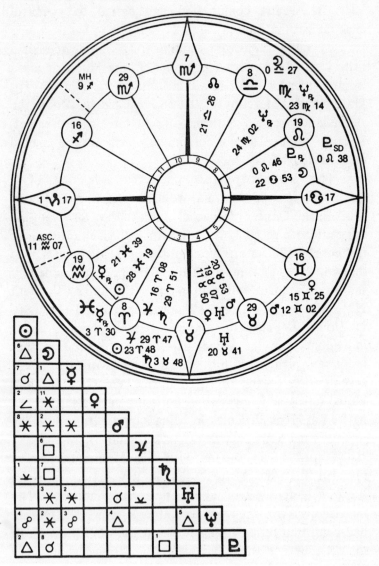

adherence to the status quo, gaining fulfillment through fantasy and secret affairs, the system was under severe challenge to set things right, to make enormous adjustments, drop defenses, begin anew.

The progressed Sun had come into exact conjunction with the radical Saturn, ruler of the Ascendant. The natal conjunction between Uranus and Mars had closed to exactness through the slight advance of progressed Uranus: a period of extremely high tension within IV, the home. —The pattern seemed to be repeating itself, with the husband taking the place of the father.

The progressed Ascendant was squaring the radical Venus in House IV (emotions in the home); was referring, in the second decanate of Aquarius, to Mercury in the fantasy axis. Progressed Saturn was square the progressed Ascendant. *Within the next year, the progressed Sun would square radical Pluto in VII,* ruler of X (personal honor and fulfillment).

The native came to this astrologer one month before her thirty-second birthday. The progressed Moon (ruling Cancer on VII) was precisely opposed her birth Sun: her fantasy-marriage-home crisis. Within the following twenty-nine months (to progressed Moon opposition with Saturn), she would have every opportunity to adjust her situation creatively. There would be an ethical, perhaps legal concern in sixteen months when the progressed Moon opposed Jupiter. Her concern would be whether to remain with her husband, perhaps get professional employment to fulfill ego ambitions, or separate from her home and begin again in a foreign country (House IX).

Example 5: Private Case
Progression for 37th year

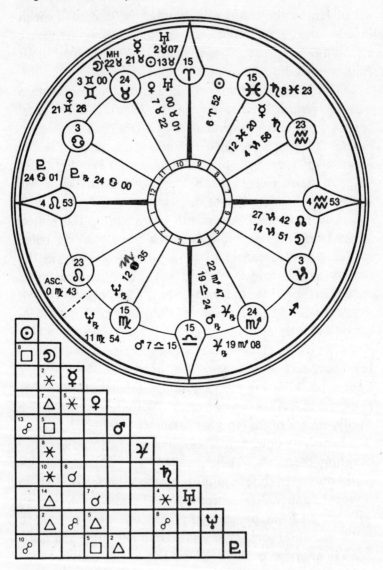

Transit measurements completed the picture, defining environmental pressures to help her make her decisions.

The pressure was to communicate (House III) with her husband and try to make adjustments within their relationship. —The woman separated from her husband and went to a foreign country. Private fantasy was more alluring than the challenge of practical cooperation and adjustment of marital perspective.

Factor-7 measurement of the Sun-Neptune opposition projects partile focus to age twenty-nine plus: the native had begun to fantasize about her unfulfilled ambitions, her personal worth (II), her unrewarding escape-marriage, and, although living in the same house with her husband, she had not had relations with him for three years at the time of consultation.

The future had hope for the very bright, attractive woman. The factor-7 measurement of the Moon-Sun trine, involving House VII so conspicuously, gives an orb of five degrees and twenty-six minutes, or an age of thirty-eight years and one month, six years after the thirty-second birthday shown in the example: the progressed Moon would be in XI trining the radical Jupiter and Saturn; the progressed Sun would be conjunct the fourth cusp.

On page 168 is the horoscope of a powerful businessman. His power is his natural drive (Sun in Aries opposed by Mars), extreme practical self-sufficiency (Earth Grand Trine: Moon in VI, Venus in X, and Neptune in II). He is a blend of administrator (Moon in Capricorn; Leo Ascendant) and mechanical inventor (Uranus-Venus conjunction in X, sextile Saturn). Both constructs are fed by a day-dreaming reliance upon imagination and fantasy (Mercury-Neptune opposition), increasing creativity but introverting practicality. His life is filled with international travel (Sun in IX; Neptune ruling Pisces on IX).

The difficulty of the horoscope is the threat of overwork: Mars retrograde symbolizes energy held back, delayed, tiring the system. The Moon makes a double-approaching square with this retrograde Mars and a double-approaching opposition with retrograde Pluto in XII. The Moon is in Capricorn in VI.

The progressions are drawn for the native's thirty-seventh year. Progressed Mars is still retrograde and applying to the exact opposition with the Sun. Mars is the ruling planet of Aries, the Sun Sign; the Sun rules Leo on the Ascendant. The several years to come would see enormous changes in his profession (Mars rules the Midheaven), his health (Ascendant) and probably his country of activity (Sun in IX). —This was precisely the native's reason for consulting this astrologer.

Five months after the progressed birthday, at the time of consultation, the progressed Moon was at 8 Gemini, applying to a square with Mercury. The progressed Moon had squared Saturn in the birthday month: the native had been heavily overworked, dangerously exhausted by efforts to expand his development, instinctively looking forward to the big shift he felt would come soon.

The progressed Moon's square to Mercury *and to Neptune* would be exact nine months later after his birthday within the progressed year. This time would be extremely important. Mercury, suggesting travel, rules Virgo on III, travel. Neptune rules Pisces on IX, foreign travel. The progressed Ascendant had just entered Virgo (trine Uranus in X), emphasizing Mercury. Progressed Mercury was opposing Jupiter (extended travel). —There was no doubt about it: the native should (would) make an extended journey beginning nine months after his birth month. The journey period(s) would probably last two to seven months until the progressed Moon quincunxed its own natal position in two months or trined the radical Mars in seven months.

The native made the trip, almost three months in length, returned home and made another trip, filling out the period. The trips were business trips designed to relax the grueling pace of developments in the home office. The native's business affairs were in good condition: progressed Sun trine natal Moon (X-VI) which overruled the progressed Midheaven opposition with Jupiter.

Without the rest trip, health conditions could have been very serious: the progressed Midheaven opposition with Jupiter could have invited over-exertion, over-speculation, over-expansion, and legal tension; the progressed Mars opposition with the Sun during work crisis could easily call into focus the natal Mars square to the Moon-Pluto opposition axis VI-XII. —The danger will still threaten the executive for several years to come, but he is taking as many precautions as he can, especially delegation of authority, the antidote for an overworked Earth Grand Trine.

Example 6: Actress
February 27, 1932; 1:30 AM; London
Progression for 41st year; date: April 7, 1932

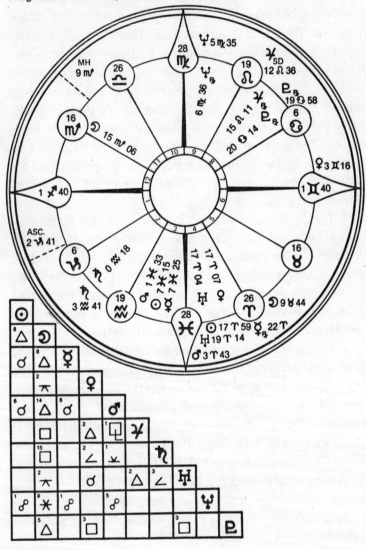

In the horoscope of an actress on page 172, the Moon in Scorpio is extremely important: in its fall; the only body non-retrograde above the horizon; squared to the Ascendant ruler Jupiter, which is retrograde in VIII (Cancer on the cusp, ruled by the Moon). It aspects every other body: trine Mercury, ruler of VII and X; trine Pluto also in VIII; wide separating trine to Mars; wide separating square to Saturn; sextile with Neptune, ruler of the Sun Sign; and quincunx (150 degrees, "developmental") with Venus and Uranus in IV. The personality's needs will be to present the emotions, deeply and profoundly, to the world, to gain recognition, support, and acceptance. The private purposes divined by the Piscean personality will elude understanding. External excesses (Moon square Jupiter) will camouflage inner wanting.

The tremendous Mars-Sun-Mercury conjunction in Pisces, square the Ascendant, exactly opposing Neptune, ruler of the Sun Sign, accentuates the sensual, the psychical, in the intuitive quadrant (northeast); the axis suggests that the whole emotional quest of the woman's personality will be in the public view as a reactor; reaction and fantasy will be the energy of the profession (Mercury rules X and VII), and will lead to multiple partnerships, marriages to find understanding (duality Sign on VII, its ruler in a duality Sign, along with the masculine symbols Mars and the Sun).

The Ascendant ruler Jupiter is in trine with the exact conjunction of Uranus and Venus. Aesthetic communication (Uranus rules III) will be an outlet for her emotions as wll as the source of her friends, her actual "home" (Uranus-Venus in IV, Neptune rules Pisces on IV); the theatricality of social and emotional expression again echoes the personality's needs and life-energy thrust. Personal drive is lacking (wide separating squares Moon-Mars, Moon-Saturn). Though in the theatre and films (Neptune opposition axis, elevation), the woman simply wants to be understood, praised for her inner privacies, to luxuriate (Moon exactly square Jupiter, ruler of the Ascendant) in the sensual. Her search for support in this need will lead through many different partners and husbands.

This is the horoscope of Elizabeth Taylor. At five years of age, pushed by a powerful mother (Uranus-Venus in IV trine Jupiter, ruler of the Ascendant, retrograde in VIII, the Self led in its projection by others, by a parent; and square Pluto in VIII: individuality and emotions under developmental tension and altered perspective through someone else's resources, limiting her self-devleopment since Pluto rules XII and is in the Moon's Sign), Elizabeth Taylor was in ballet school (progressed Moon opposed Pluto); at ten, with the progressed New Moon at 16 Pisces in III, trine Pluto and the Moon, and the progressed Moon crossing IV, she was put into films. —At a very early age, her personal potentials were controlled by others, precociously expanded into make-believe, theatricality, sensuality, and an unusual home and social framework to say the least. A series of marriages to celebrities began early, extending the absorption of personality by others.

Elizabeth Taylor married Richard Burton in 1964 at thirty-two (her fifth husband). Burton is a Scorpio (10

November 1925) with his birth Sun and Saturn conjunct her Moon, his Mercury conjunct her Ascendant, his Moon conjunct her Neptune, opposing her Mars-Sun-Mercury: Burton took over management of her life totally. He provided the support, the thinking, the luxuries, the fulfillment of fantasies, until separation on 4 July 1973 and the announcement of divorce plans on 1 August 1973.

The progressions in Elizabeth Taylor's horoscope are drawn for her forty-first year, 1973 to 1974 (birth: 27 February 1932, 1:30 AM, London; SP date: April 7, +13:30 hours increment). It is so obvious: the progressed Sun is exactly conjunct Uranus-Venus, applying to the square with Pluto; Venus has progressed to conjunction with the seventh cusp, square Mars, applying to squares with Neptune, Sun, and Mercury. And perhaps most important, progressed Jupiter has in this year *resumed direct motion,* i.e., "stationary-direct."

Tremendous tensions of individual assertion had developed within the actress during the preceding two years: *progressed New Moon* at 16 Aries, conjunct Uranus, trine Jupiter, quincunx Moon, one year before. She surely saw her *own* way for the first time in her life; Jupiter, ruler of her Ascendant, shifted the emotional counterpoint that had ruled her life into direct personal assertion. This is emphasized by the position of the progressed Moon at the time of separation five months after her forty-first birthday: 14 Taurus, in awareness opposition to the radical Moon and exactly square Jupiter! Her period of turmoil was in the three months between the progressed Moon's square to progressed Jupiter, "stationary-direct" at the first terminal three months after her birthday, and announcement of separation three degrees (months) later at the square to radical Jupiter, the second terminal.

There had been rumors of arguments and threats of separation earlier, throughout the last five years, as Mars was crossing the fourth cusp, indicating shifts of home.

But for how long will Elizabeth Taylor be able to be alone in her world? Might she marry on the rebound once again (progressed Sun conjunct Venus in the Venus-Uranus conjunction; Mercury retrograding)? Jupiter *transits* the Mars-Sun-Mercury conjunction in April 1974, a time of tremendous personal opportunity. Might a sympathetic friend offer her a grand opportunity to start again?

What might happen when the progressed Moon comes to the seventh cusp as progressed Venus squares Sun-Mercury late in 1977? In *retrogradation,* progressed Mercury, ruler of VII, conjoins Venus-Uranus; the progressed Midheaven conjoins the Moon, and the progressed Moon will be conjunct Pluto and Jupiter when she is forty-eight, in 1980. —These will be important times for Elizabeth Taylor. The reader might like to make an interpretation of these progressions and watch for corroborating developments!

Additional observations: progressed Moon paralleled progressed Mars; the progressed Sun paralleled progressed Uranus. In the radical horoscope, only Uranus and Venus are in an Angle. By factor-7 approximation, the exact Mars conjunction with Sun-Mercury is forty-one years and two months! By radix direction at forty-one, Neptune opposes

Uranus-Venus; Pluto opposes Mars. —Elizabeth Taylor's individuality crisis is amply corroborated.

7

Limits of Progression

The straight lines of deduction approximate ever so finely the arc of the whole; yet, radix directions and Secondary Progressions still always remain approximations... they are limited. Something is missing.

There are other progression systems, lines of deduction, in astrological technique. R. C. Davison takes Secondary Progressions further, equating weekly and montly progressions to years of life. There is the system of lunation progressions, measuring each successive lunation after birth as a chart for the progressed year. As we have seen, there are converse directions and progressions, measuring movement development backwards. In the next volume of this series, solar revolution charts will be studied. —These other systems "add decimal places" to the astrological constant of intra-horoscope relationships. The system one day equals one year seems to work the most satisfactorily.

All the progression systems concentrate upon the internal development of the radix. Various approaches are made to capture somehow the individual development schedule promised by the application and separation of radical aspects, by the forming of new aspects related to the imprint of birth, by the change of personal time and development space within the constant flow of objective time.

What *is* missing in our studies so far is *a measurement of the environment*. The birth horoscope lives among the horoscope development-schemes of others. Time and space are shared. The individual horoscope must be studied in relation to factors outside its personal portion of time and space. The time within must relate to the time without. The environment is within *actual* time, defined by transit development of the planets in the present. Progressions will indicate internal potentials and transits will indicate external challenge. Together, behavioral response is indicated, identity is formed; the individual finds his place within the inexorable flow of time.

With the integration of transit theory, progressions become *potentials* of response. Progressions become the transition between subjective inclination and objective demand. The whole of personality emerges into actuality.

Indeed, transit theory itself becomes another approximation in relation to the fulfillment of creative structure. Together with radix potentials and progression preparedness, the number of possibilities of interpretation become almost incomprehensibly vast. Within the individual human being, however, the possibilities order themselves naturally around a focal center of identity, social framework, free will assertion, and goal fulfillment. It is in the "nature of a miracle," the mode of which surpasses the human understanding, how the systems unify, how the possibilities integrate within the whole, how the whole emerges to satisfy astrological measurement, the study of man, and the service to development.

Older teachings often stated that no event of significance can occur in the life without a major progressed aspect involving the Sun. This is simply not so in modern times. Many more opportunities are open to the individual: travel, education, specialization. One can go away from a problem, learn more how to solve it, or gain specialized control over it. Medicines alter the effects of disease; psychology can alter the mind; religion and philosophy can sustain the spirit; history clarifies perspective. The developing Sun distributes its light more powerfully in modern times than ever before. The illumination of the whole is more vast in the modern horoscope and, at the same time, easier to appreciate in its nuance. Heterogeneity of personal expression is now the rule; change and development are incredibly accelerated.

Progressions indicate enormous nuance of potential, related to the birth horoscope, structured within the development of horoscope time. The personality, prepared in individual diversity, meets the environment in a wholly modern way. The birth horoscope subdivides more easily today; the central focus of illumination shifts often during the lifetime; new wholes of personality emerge, new "presents." In studying such dynamic change, the astrologer wields many different analytical systems. In recognition of the diverse potentials and challenges of modern times, perhaps we now have the hypothesis that no event of significance occurs in the life without *several* measurements suggesting it. We shall see in Volumes VII and VIII.

The birth horoscope indicates the innate potential for specific development. Radix inspection and progressions suggest the time scheme of the development. Then transit theory (Volume VII) must bring external challenge to internal potential at the right time. —In the study of integrated transits, a pattern of interwoven measurements will emerge to justify the "nature of the miracle."

All prediction systems work to eliminate somehow the inexactness, the factor of indeterminateness between man's measurements and nature's symbolism. Every astrologer finds his own way to expand the birth present. A band of meaning wraps itself around the linear flow of life-time. There is a slight, elusive twist in the band that introduces the mystery of life and time.

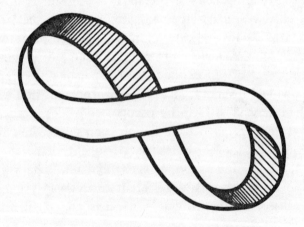

In mathemathics, we have the Moebius strip phenomenon. We can take a strip of paper, twist it once, and bind the ends. Then, by cutting into the band longitudinally for its entire circumference, we have at the end of the process one whole, grander circle! —What has happened? Man's incision has given birth to an even greater whole, and then another, and another, and another . . . .

Appendix

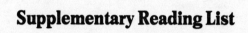

Supplementary Reading List

Davison, R. C. *The Technique of Prediction.* New York: Samuel Weiser.

De Luce, Robert. *Complete Method of Prediction.* Los Angeles: De Luce Co.

Doane, Doris Chase. *Astrology: 30 Years Research.* Hollywood: Professional Astrologers, Inc., 1956.

Moore, Marcia and Mark Douglas. *Astrology in Action.* York Harbor, Maine: Arcane Publications, 1970.

Rudhyar, Dane. *The Lunation Cycle.* Berkeley, California: Shambala Publications, 1971.

Smith, Alson J. *Immortality: The Scientific Evidence.* New York: Signet Publications, The New American Library.

The Davison book deals with Secondary Progressions; the De Luce book is advanced, dealing with trigonometric primary directions. The Doane book is currently available through Llewellyn Publications, Box 3383, St. Paul, Minnesota, 55165.

For the volumes that follow in this series and for all future work in prediction, the student will need a small booklet table of planetary positions: *The Geocentric Longitudes and Declinations of Neptune, Herschel, Saturn, Jupiter, and Mars, 1900 to 2001* by Raphael (London: Foulsham).

The Principles and Practice of Astrology
for home study and college curriculum
by Noel Tyl
in twelve volumes

I. Horoscope Construction

Here is an unrivaled explanation of the construction of a horoscope. All time and position corrections are made maximally clear. A totally self-contained volume, with tables and practice horoscope blanks. Contents include: calculating the time of birth—step-by-step guidance, use of materials and examples; measuring the houses—what they are, how they're placed; the calligraphy—the symbols of astrology, meaning of the signs, illustrative birthdays of famous people; placing the planets—measuring planetary movement, test horoscopes; calculation review—special time problems explained; the Sun and the signs—the Sun as the key, Sun Sign interpretations, the elements, polarities, modes; the ruling planets—meaning and function of planets in the chart with sample horoscopes reviewed; the Age of Aquarius—what it is and what it means to astrologers.

II. The Houses: Their Signs and Planets

The rationale of house demarcation, the meanings of the signs upon each house, the planets' significance in every house; derivative house readings.

III. The Planets: Their Signs and Aspects

A full expansion of the elements and modes in a refreshingly modern style; the significance of every planet within every sign; the reading of aspects and dignities "at a glance"; the suggested meanings of all major aspects and Sun-Moon combinations. An invaluable master reference book for horoscope interpretation.

IV. Aspects and Houses in Analysis

Analytical synthesis technique presented through many examples, showing hemisphere emphasis, retrogradation patterns, the grand trine, the grand square, the T square in complete explanation, the lunar nodal axis, parallels of declination, and the part of fortune; the "law of naturalness." A volume devoted totally to the art of synthesis.

V. Astrology and Personality

Never before presented: an explanation of psychological theories of personality translated into astrological terms and technique! The theories of Kurt Lewin, Carl Jung, Henry Murray, Abraham Maslow, Erich Fromm, Alfred Adler and Sigmund Freud; and astrological glossary of psychological terms and personality traits.

VI. The Expanded Present

An introduction to prediction, an analysis of the time dimension in astrology; application and separation of aspects, "rapport" measurements, secondary progression, primary directions, "factor 7" analysis. Many examples clarify the work of astrology toward understanding change and development in personality, within free-will and fate.

VII. Integrated Transits

A definitive work, modernizing the rationale, analysis and application of transit theory, in accord with the needs and expectations of modern people. Astrology is translated into behavior with many real-life examples for every major transit. The work also includes studies of solar revolution, rectification, eclipse theory, and accidents.

VIII. Analysis and Prediction

A gallery of astrological portraits: the whole-view of astrological analysis; inspection of the past, expansion of the present, the creation of the future. Each step of deduction, analysis, and projection is presented in the sharing of real-life horoscopes: *you* become the astrologer! Radix methods, progressions, and transits are fully interpreted. In addition, there is an introduction to Horary and Electional Astrology.

IX. Special Horoscope Dimensions

Success: vocation, relocation, opportunity, elections. Sex: chart comparison, sex profile, love, homosexuality, abortion, creativity. Illness: health problems, surgery, vitality.

X. Astrological Counsel

Never before presented: a full, detailed inspection of the psychodynamics of the astrologer-client relationship, with examples showing the astrologer's consideration of the horoscope *and* the individual, bringing together the personality and its time structure for fulfillment. Difficulties analyzed, communication techniques explored.

XI. Astrology: Astral, Mundane, Occult

The fixed stars, the individual degrees and decanates; considerations of mundane astrology governing international events; study of death and reincarnation, the areas shared by astrology and occult studies.

XII. Times to Come

A projection of astrology into the future, investigating the potential of astrology. A complete subject index for all twelve volumes.

Teacher's Guide

Not part of the series, but for educators teaching astrology. A complete explanation of all subjects: difficulties, suggested techniques, test examinations for each step of development.

The Horoscope as Identity   **Price $10.00**

Studies in the Astrology of Sex, Ambition, and Identity within modern, freer times.   **by Noel Tyl**

What the publisher says:

If this is truly a New Age that we have entered, the Age of Aquarius, then there must be new things said: new interpretations of the Ancient Wisdom of which we are the guardians.

At Llewellyn we receive an average of one manuscript every day—most of them saying nothing, some of them saying old things in new ways, some of them publishable. For a cycle of twelve years I waited to see a manuscript that said something new in astrology—and I waited in vain. I did not see a single astrological book meeting that ideal until the exact completion of that twelve-year cycle in February of 1973—and then it happened!

As far as Llewellyn is concerned, a new star was born on the day that I completed reading the manuscript of *The Horoscope as Identity*.

The author of this book actually incarnates the new influx of psychological meaning in terms of astrological practice that this Age demands. He speaks to the needs of the present and coming student of astrology and psychology combined as they should be.

This is not a book of tables, or a repetition of what is said well or poorly in so many other books. It is not a book that sees astrology as frozen in medieval times and meanings. It is a book for both the advanced student of astrology and the intelligent layman who wants to see what is really in modern astrology. It is a book for the reader who is ready to be liberated—who will be able to use the knowledge of self and this world to achieve freedom and mastery of his destiny that is the goal of all astrological and psychological analysis.

The particular value of this book is the modern understanding of Saturn in the chart, the concept of the sex-profile, and the guidance to speed-reading the horoscope. Case studies include: Albert Speer, Hitler's architect; a famous businessman (survival or death); Judy Garland.

Fifty-eight horoscope charts illustrate the text.